Mt. Rainier Trails

125 hikes at Mt. Rainier National Park

Paul Hodge

Sound & Mountains Publishing

Mt. Rainier Trails

Published by **Sound & Mountains Publishing**

Text, photographs and maps are by Paul Hodge

All trail guide books should point out that a guide to any enterprise that involves physical activity cannot be responsible for how that activity is carried out. Trail travelers always must use care, must be knowledgable and skilled in outdoor adventure activity and must be prepared for unexpected conditions. The author and publisher are not responsible for any problem that may arise from the use of this book or of these trails.

Front cover: Mt. Rainier from Tolmie Peak (Hike 104)
Back Cover: Emmons Glacier and the summit from Mt. Fremont (Hike 76)

ISBN 0-9753496-4-3

Sound & Mountains Publishing is a publisher of books about the trails and other features of the mountains, lowlands and islands of the Puget Sound region of Washington State. For information about other books published or in production write to

Sound & Mountains Publishing
4727 Ravenna Ave. N. E., Suite 101
Seattle, WA 98105-4165

TABLE OF CONTENTS

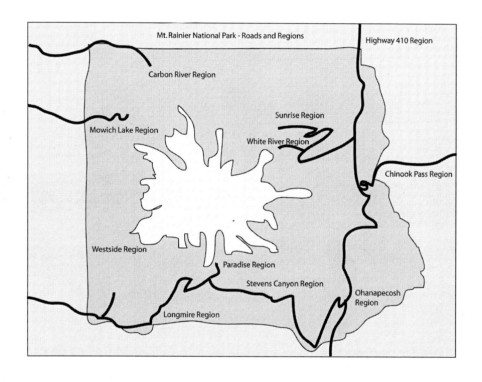

Map 1 Roads and Regions

Table of Hikes

Note: Mileages quoted are for round trips and may vary depending on the exact starting and turn-around points. In some cases slightly different routes are possible. For the Westside Road hikes, mileages quoted are from the road. Transportation to the trailhead is not included.

Hike Number	Hike Name	Miles (RT)	Trailhead Elevation (feet)	Difficulty
Longmire Region				
1	Kautz Creek Nature Trail	0.1	2400	Easy
2	Indian Henry's via Kautz	11.2	2400	Strenuous
3	Twin Firs Nature Trail	0.4	2420	Easy
4	Trail of the Shadows	0.7	2750	Easy
5	Longmire - Cougar Rock	4.0	2750	Moderate
6	Rampart Ridge Loop	4.8	2750	Moderate
7	Rampart to Indian Henry	12.5	2800	Strenuous
8	Van Trump via Rampart	9.0	2800	Strenuous
9	Eagle Peak	7.0	2750	Strenuous
10	Carter Falls	2.2	3200	Easy
11	Cougar Rock to Narada	6.0	3200	Moderate
12	Comet Falls	3.8	3600	Moderate
13	Van Trump via Falls	5.8	3600	Strenuous
14	Mildred Point via Falls	9.0	3600	Strenuous
Paradise Region				
15	Nisqually Vista	1.2	5400	Easy
16	Myrtle Falls	1.0	5400	Easy
17	Alta Vista	1.5	5400	Easy
18	Dead Horse Creek	1.0	5400	Easy
19	Moraine Trail	2.0	5870	Moderate
20	Skyline Trail	5.2	5400	Moderate
21	Pebble Creek	0.7	6600	Easy
22	Golden Gate	3.2	6400	Moderate
23	Paradise Glacier Trail	2.8	6000	Moderate
24	Camp Muir	8.6	5400	Strenuous
25	Sluiskin Falls Loop	3.3	5400	Moderate
26	Lakes Trail	4.5	5400	Moderate
Stevens Canyon				
27	High Lakes Trail Loop	2.7	4900	Moderate
28	Faraway Rock	1.5	4900	Easy
29	Narada Falls-Lakes Loop	2.6	4450	Moderate
30	Pinnacle Peak	2.6	4900	Moderate

31	Plummer Peak	3.5	4900	Strenuous
32	Bench and Snow Lakes	2.5	4500	Easy
33	Martha Falls	2.0	4140	Easy
34	Box Canyon Loop	1.5	3100	Easy
35	Nickel Creek Camp	1.6	3100	Easy
36	Cowlitz Divide	9.0	3100	Strenuous
37	Backbone Ridge	3.0	3400	Strenuous
38	Backbone Lake	6.0	3400	Moderate
Ohanapecosh Region				
39	Grove of the Patriarchs	1.3	2250	Easy
40	Hot Springs Nature Trail	0.6	2000	Easy
41	Silver Falls Loop	2.7	2000	Moderate
42	Laughingwater Trail	12.0	2200	Strenuous
43	Eastside Trail	14.0	2250	Moderate
44	Ollalie Creek Camp	7.6	2300	Moderate
45	Shriner Peak	8.4	2400	Strenuous
46	Deer Creek Falls	0.8	3200	Easy
47	Kotsuck Falls	3.0	3200	Moderate
Chinook Pass Region				
48	Cayuse to Chinook	3.0	4600	Moderate
49	Upper Eastside	7.4	4600	Moderate
50	Tipsoo Lakes Loop	0.5	5300	Easy
51	Naches Peak Loop	5.0	5400	Moderate
52	Dewey Lakes	5.0	5400	Moderate
53	Deadwood Lakes	4.0	5250	Moderate
54	Sheep Lake	3.8	5400	Moderate
55	Sourdough Gap	6.4	5400	Moderate
56	Crystal Peak	8.0	3500	Moderate
57	Crystal Lakes	6.6	3500	Moderate
White River Region				
58	Owyhigh Lakes	7.0	3700	Moderate
59	Summerland	8.4	3800	Moderate
60	Panhandle Gap	11.2	3800	Strenuous
61	Indian Bar	17.6	3800	Strenuous
62	White River Loop	0.5	4300	Easy
63	Emmons Moraine Trail	5.8	4300	Moderate
64	Glacier Basin	7.0	4300	Moderate
65	White River - Borroughs	12.5	4300	Strenuous
Sunrise Region				
66	Sunrise Lake	1.2	6100	Easy
67	Palisades Lakes	7.0	6100	Moderate
68	Hidden Lake	6.2	6100	Moderate
69	Sourdough Ridge Trail	6.0	6400	Moderate
70	Dege Peak	0.6	6800	Easy
71	Shadow Lake	2.4	6400	Easy

72	Emmons Overlook	3.0	6400	Moderate
73	Emmons Vista	0.6	6400	Easy
74	Silver Forest	3.0	6400	Easy
75	Frozen Lake	2.8	6400	Moderate
76	Mt. Fremont Lookout	5.4	640	Moderate
77	Burroughs Mountain	6.0	6400	Moderate
78	Nothern Loop	18.3	6400	Strenuous
79	Berkeley Park	7.6	6400	Moderate
80	Grand Park	13.0	6400	Strenuous
81	Forest Lake	5.0	6400	Moderate
82	Huckleberry Creek	20.0	6400	Strenuous
83	Skyscraper Mountain	7.4	6400	Moderate
84	Mystic Lake	17.4	6400	Strenuous
85	Lake Eleanor	20.0	6400	Strenuous
Carbon River Region				
86	West Boundary Trail	18.0	1800	Strenuous
87	June Creek Nature Trail	0.3	1800	Easy
88	Green Lake	4.0	2100	Moderate
89	Chenuis Falls	0.4	2150	Easy
90	Tirzah Peak	4.0	2150	Moderate
91	Carbon River Loop	6.0	2400	Moderate
92	Carbon Glacier	7.0	2400	Moderate
93	Moraine Park	13.0	2400	Strenuous
94	Windy Gap	12.0	2400	Strenuous
95	Natural Bridge	2.0	5700	Moderate
96	Lake James	16.4	2400	Strenuous
97	Ipsut Pass	7.8	2400	Strenuous
98	Cataract Camp	8.6	2400	Moderate
99	Seattle Park	12	2400	Strenuous
Mowich Lake Region				
100	Paul Peak Trail	6.2	3700	Moderate
101	Mowich River Loop	8.5	3700	Strenuous
102	Grindstone Trail	2.5	4300	Easy
103	Eunice Lake	5.0	5000	Moderate
104	Tolmie Peak Lookout	6.4	5000	Moderate
105	Spray Falls	4.2	5000	Easy
106	Spray Park	8.0	5000	Moderate
107	Sunset Park	20	5000	Strenuous
Westside Road Region				
108	Lake George	2.0	3900	Easy
109	Gobbler's Knob	4.0	3900	Moderate
110	Goat Lake	8.0	3900	Moderate
111	Round Pass Cutoff	2.0	3900	Easy
112	Tahoma Creek Bridge	4.4	3200	Moderate
113	Indian Henry's	7.0	3200	Moderate

114	Mirror Lakes	1.8	5500	Easy
115	Emerald Ridge	7.8	3500	Moderate
116	Klapatche Park	5.0	3800	Moderate
117	St. Andrews Park	7.4	3800	Moderate
Highway 410 Region				
118	Suntop Lookout	2.0	4750	Easy
119	Fawn Ridge	16.0	4750	Strenuous
129	Doe Falls	1.0	4150	Easy
121	Crystal Mountain Trails	various	4800	various
122	Camp Sheppard Trails	various	2400	various
123	Riverbank Trails	various	2400	various
124	Federation Forest Trails	various	1550	various
Wonderland Trail				
125	The Wonderland Trail	92-100	2750	strenuous

List of Maps

Chapter 1 – Introduction

About this Guide

Mt. Rainier National Park is one of the best in the Park system for summer hiking. There are glorious hiking trips on hundreds of miles of well-maintained trails, from deep lowland forest to high sub-arctic tundra. Rather than covering only a selected group of trails, this guide aims to be comprehensive. It describes **all** trails in the Park, as well as many that are just outside the Park's boundaries. In addition to the popular well-known trails there are some nice trails that are seldom hiked, including some that are abandoned but still hikable. A hiker can find just about any kind of trail that she or he might be thirsting for among the 125 different hiking trips included here.

The book divides the Mt. Rainier area into 12 regions, mainly based on access roads (map pg. 6). It begins at the southwest corner, where most visitors enter the Park, and continues around the mountain in a counterclockwise direction. There are about 10 trails described for each region, except for Chapter 13 on the Wonderland Trail, which is divided into 10 days. Each trail is about the right length for a day hike, though a few are short enough for only a brief stroll. All are well worth the effort.

Getting Started

The trails of Mt. Rainier are a glorious resource. They can provide years of pleasurable hiking. But before heading for the mountain, there are various things that should be considered. First, we must point out that mountain hiking is a strenuous undertaking and can be dangerous under certain circumstances. Mountain weather can be unpredictable; a sunny morning can turn into a stormy or even a snowy afternoon. Some trails are steep and involve traveling along the edges of formidable cliff tops. No-one should proceed on a trail trip without tiptop health and good judgment. Experience in navigating in the woods is valuable and skill in map reading is important. THE PUBLISHER AND AUTHOR ARE NOT RESPONSIBLE FOR ANY KIND OF MISADVENTURE THAT USERS OF THIS BOOK MAY EXPERIENCE.

The Ten Essentials

The Mountaineers club of Seattle has long promoted the concept of the "ten essentials", things that everyone should take with them into the mountains. The classical list is as follows:

Map	Headlamp or flashlight
Compass	First-aid kit
Sunglasses	Fire starter
Extra food	Matches
Extra clothing	Knife

Land of Eternal Sunshine?

Some words about the weather: it's not always sunny at Mt. Rainer. Almost all of the photographs in this book were taken in bright sunshine. Frequently the summer weather is different from that, - there can be fog, rain and even snow. Seattle can be basking on a warm sunshiny day and the poor folks up at Paradise can find themselves deep in a cloud, thoroughly white-outed. But not all hikes at Rainier need to be fair-weather trips. There are several nice hikes in this book that can be enjoyed even when the mountain is not "out". Here is a list of suggestions:

Cloudy Day Hikes

1 Kautz Creek Nature Trail
3 Twin Firs Nature Trail
4 Trail of the Shadows
5 Longmire to Cougar Rock
6 Rampart Ridge Loop
10 Carter Falls
11 Cougar Rock to Narada Falls
12 Comet Falls
27 High Lakes Trail Loop
29 Narada Falls - Lakes Loop
33 Martha Falls
34 Box Canyon Loop
35 Nickel Creek Camp
37 Backbone Ridge
38 Backbone Lake
39 Grove of the Patriarchs
40 Hot Springs Nature Trail
41 Silver Falls Loop
43 Eastside Trail

44 Ollalie Creek Camp
46 Deer Creek Falls
47 Kotsuck Falls
48 Cayuse – Chinook Trail
49 Upper Eastside Trail
62 White River Loop
87 June Creek Nature Trail
88 Green Lake
89 Chenuis Falls
91 Carbon River Loop
98 Cataract Camp
100 Paul Peak Trail
101 Mowich River Loop
102 Grindstone Trail
108 Lake George
122 Camp Sheppard Area Trails
123 Riverbank Trails
124 Federation Forest Trails

Maps

The first of the ten essentials listed above is **map**. One should never venture out without a map. For guidance in planning a trip, we include 16 maps in this book, but we believe that a hiker should also always have a large-scale, detailed topographic map in his pack.

There are many excellent maps of Mt. Rainier National Park and some can be purchased at shops within the Park. They are also available at bookstores and outdoor stores in the region. The following are maps that we especially like:

Mt. Rainier 7.5 minute quadrangles, published by the US Geological Survey. There are 8 separate topographic maps that cover most of the Park. They are large-scale and beautifully detailed.

Green Trails maps. Nos. 269 and 270 cover most of the Park, but it's also a good idea to obtain Greenwater (238), Bumping Lake (271), Randle (301) and Packwood (302) to have all of the regions discussed in this book, as small amounts of the Park appear on those maps. Green Trails maps can be found at most stores near the park or in bookstores and outdoor stores in the urban areas of the region.

Mt. Rainier National Park Trip Planning Guides. There are three of these, based (as are all of the maps in this list) on USGS topographic maps. There are three separate maps and they include brief descriptions of the principle trails in each region. They are published by the Pacific Northwest National Parks and Forests Association and are available at shops in the Park.

Hiking Map and Guide – Mt. Rainier National Park. Published by Earthwalk Press, the large map (27x30 inches) is available in a waterproof edition. Included are brief trail descriptions and close-up inset maps of the Paradise and Sunrise regions.

Books

This is not the only book about Mt. Rainier. There are dozens of others, many of them hiking guides. We'd like to list all of the books about the mountain, but will limit this list to those that we think are outstanding.

Filley, Bette. **Discovering the Wonders of the Wonderland Trail** (Dunamis House). This is a remarkably complete and enjoyable volume entirely devoted to Mt. Rainier's premiere trail.

Judd, Ron. **Day Hike! Mount Rainier** (Sasquatch Books). This volume has good descriptions of the shorter trail trips and some excellent black and white photographs.

Schneider, Heidi and Mary Skjelset. **Hiking Mt. Rainier National Park** (Falcon Publishing). This is a particularly nice guide, well organized and relatively complete. The text is good; the photographs are serviceable.

Smoot, Jeff. **Adventure Guide to Mount Rainier** (Chockstone Press). The principle hiking trails are described, but the unusual feature of this guide is the inclusion of many off-trail trips, as well as climbing and ski-touring routes.

Spring, Ira and Harvey Manning. **50 Hikes in Mount Rainier National Park** (The Mountaineers). The best-known guide to the Park, "50 Hikes" has been through several editions since it first came out in 1969. The photographs are superb and the text is brief but authoritative.

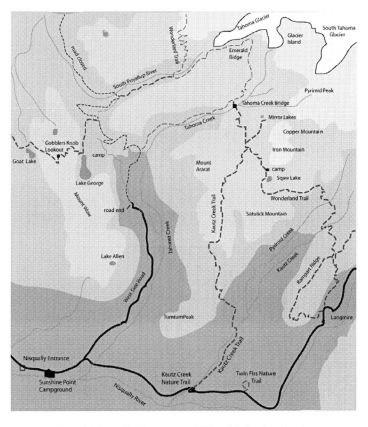

Map 2 Nisqually Entrance and Westside Region South

Chapter 2 - The Longmire Region

Most people enter the Park at the southwest corner, where the Nisqually Entrance welcomes millions of visitors a year. Before reaching the entrance, the highway passes through a typical "pioneer" countryside, with stump farms, cabin courts, log inns, resorts, restaurants, houses with yards resembling junk heaps, some historic old railroad equipment and a large artificial lake. After this, the entrance to the Park provides a marvelous change. Here, after paying a fee to a ranger and receiving a map and information package, one enters a different world. The sky is full of the tops of giant trees, trees that have been here for hundreds or even thousands of years, and the views beyond the road include meadows splashed in sunlight and the dark forest floor, where wild lilies and orchids add color to the quiet shadows.

The southwest corner of the Park is dominated by the "village" of Longmire, named after the pionering family who first settled here. There is an inn, a museum, a shop and a ranger station where information and permits can be obtained. The National Park Inn, a handsome historic landmark, has pleasant rooms and a restaurant.

There are two campgrounds in this part of the Park. The first to be encountered, the small Sunshine Point Campground, is only a half mile inside the entrance, set in a grove of firs and deciduous trees next to a wide stretch of the Nisqually River's gravelly bed. There is also a picnic area, set right up close to the river's rocky bank. The other nearby campground is 2 miles above Longmire, just off the Paradise Road, and makes a nice off-season trail trip from Longmire (Trail 5).

Open all year, Longmire, at an elevation of 2800 feet, is only infrequently buried in snow and is an excellent center of off-season trail trips. Some of these trails start right at the village and others have trailheads nearby. We include in this section trails that start anywhere from the Park Entrance to about half-way up the Paradise Road past Longmire.

map pg. 15

For visitors entering the Park at the Nisqually Entrance, the first opportunity to stop, get out of the car and walk is at the Kautz Creek Washout area, where there is a short trail through a remarkable example of the violence of the mountain environment. In October, 1947, a huge wall of water and mud rushed down from the Kautz Glacier, tearing out a new canyon in the upper Kautz Creek Valley and spreading out in the lower valley, knocking trees down and destroying the forest. The highway bridge was swept away and a large chunk of the road disappeared. The cause of this sudden flood was found to be a circumstance that sometimes happens with glaciers. A mud and ice dam had formed near the terminus of the glacier, blocking the melting water, which formed a lake-like reservoir. Following torrential rains the dam broke and a huge amount of water and mud flowed violently down the valley, creating the Kautz Creek Washout and isolating the people at Longmire from the world for weeks.

The trail here is a very short one, but it has some interesting features. Starting across the road from the parking area, the trail is only a few hundred yards long. It travels through the new forest that is growing up where the washout destroyed the old. The trail is one of the few that are accessible to wheelchairs and its plank surface was built of recycled plastic, made to look like wood. Construction of the trail was aided by a group of Japanese school-age volunteers. Signs along the way explain both the history of the washout and the interesting history of the construction of the trail.

The trail ends at a viewpoint, where one looks up the valley of devastation towards the mountain. In the foreground are the new trees that are growing rapidly, soon to rob the visitor of the mountain view.

It's not just interesting to see how powerfully destructive such a flood can be, but also to see how nature reforests itself. No trees were planted here after the food; all were naturally reseeded. First deciduous trees (willows, alders) sprang up and later evergreens (Douglas Firs, Western Red Cedars) took their place. These two photographs show the difference only 50 years have made.

1950

2000

Indian Henry's Hunting Ground is the romantic name for a spectacular alpine parkland on the southwest flanks of the mountain. It was named for a person whose "Boston name" was Indian Henry, but whose Indian name was Sootoolick. A farmer who hosted and guided early climbers of Rainier, Sootoolick was especially well acquainted with the forested slopes of the mountain. The wonderful parkland named for him is marked by extensive, rolling fields of flowers, especially lupine, and small lakes that reflect the rugged view of Rainier seen from this angle.

The trail from Kautz Creek to Indian Henry's is a fairly long one (5.6 miles one way), but is well worth the effort, as it is full of variety and inspiring views, which come towards the end. The elevation gain is substantial, 3200 feet to the high point reached prior to Indian Henry's, making this a fairly strenuous day hike.

The trail leaves from the main south entrance road, about half way between the Nisqually entrance and Longmire. The trailhead is just past the bridge over Kautz Creek, where there's a parking area and a display regarding the Kautz Creek washout (see Trail 1).

The trail begins along the now quiet creek, passing through a young forest that has grown up after the devastation of 1947, so the trees are all only youngsters, 50 or so years old. The first mile of trail travels north towards the heights, but is nearly level. On a hot summer day the thick young woods provide a pleasantly cool start. After this pleasant mile the trail turns left and crosses Kautz Creek. The log bridges across the creek are frequently washed away in the spring and have to be replaced, an annual nuisance for the trail crews. They're usually in place well before the high country opens up, however.

Shortly after the creek crossing the trail begins its long ascent, with many switchbacks carrying hikers up through deep virgin forest. Like most lowland forests in the park, this one is a fine example of luxurious old growth, full of giant firs and hemlocks with an open understory marked by occasional clusters of members of the orchid family.

One sees a lot of forest on this part of the trip and only occasionally does a window open up to show more distant views. Some of these give the hiker a brief view of another destination, Eagle Peak (Trail 9) and its neighbors in the Tatoosh Range.

About a mile from the Kautz Creek crossing a small side creek is crossed, not far from its headwaters in a narrow valley. No more creeks are encountered on the hike. The trail leaves that small valley, angles up the south slopes of an unnamed minor peak, then switchbacks steeply up to the east. At the top of these giant stair-like switchbacks the trail levels a little and comes to an open area, proceeding more gradually through patches of forest and flowery meadows, an appetizer for what is to come.

19

From here on the ascent is more gradual and the views open up. The trail winds its way up a valley between two 5000 foot peaks, with the forest much changed from what was found below. Here subalpine trees predominate, including Pacific Silver Fir and Noble Fir, both looking very much like the Christmas trees sold in vacant lots in the city (these species are often grown by Christmas tree farmers). These trees in turn are replaced with the higher elevation trees: Alaska Cedar, Mountain Hemlock and Subalpine Fir.

The trail's progress is a pleasant one through this natural parkland but this is Mt. Rainier National Park, after all, and where is Mt. Rainier? Soon the forest opens completely to the north and the Mountain appears.

This is an unusual view of Rainier. From here it appears to be a pointy mountain, with a high rocky summit and a secondary peak on its left. But the view is misleading. The pointed summit is not the top of the mountain but a secondary peak itself, misnamed Point Success. A climber reaching its top will find that real success is still over 3000 horizontal and 250 vertical feet to the north, at Columbia Crest, Rainier's true summit. That snowy feature is not visible from here, as it is hiding behind the bulk of Point Success.

The peak to the left of Point Success from this viewpoint is called Liberty Cap. It is the third of Rainier's three high points and is about 50 feet lower in elevation than Point Success. The concave region of glaciers and rock between Liberty Cap and Point Success is the Sunset Amphitheater, a well-named feature, as it is glorious at sunset, when its

20

frosting of snow and ice glows red in the last rays of sunlight, then soft pink in the alpenglow.

As the trail continues, views also open up to the east. The rugged west wall of Satulick Mountain dominates the foreground. It has the appearance of a series of huge rough pillars, fringed on the top with trees and buttressed at the bottom with talus. It is possible to discern the layering of the volcanic flows that formed this mountain, now scoured by ice and worn away by a stream.

To the left of the trail is another peak, called Mount Ararat. James Longmire is said to have discovered relics here of an ancient ship and concluded that Noah certainly must have landed his Arc at this place. No doubt this story, like Longmire's others, formed part of the entertainment he provided the guests of his hotel. The trail passes close below Mt. Ararat's 6000 foot summit.

As the trail goes higher, more distant mountains become visible on the horizon. Off to the south it is usually possible to make out the stub of once-beautiful Mount St. Helens. It's almost lost in the jumble of foothills, but is identifiable by its near-symmetry (and sometimes by the cloud of steam rising from its crater).

A better-behaved mountain, properly covered by glaciers and snow, lies to the east of St. Helens and at a little greater distance. It is Mt. Adams, only 2000 feet shorter than Rainier, but much less famous. Its symmetrical dome-shaped form is conspicuous to the southeast. Like Rainier, Mt. Adams is a composite volcano, made up of both lava and volcanic ash. It has several spectacular glaciers and is surrounded by a dryer, more open forest than Rainier's, so that its alpine parklands are more desert-like, though quite beautiful where they have been preserved. Unlike Rainier and St. Helens, Mt. Adams is not in a national park or monument. Part of it lies in a National Forest Wilderness area and part is in the Yakima Indian Reservation.

The uplands here are often colorful. In the meadows avalanche lilies quickly follow the melting of the snow in the spring (usually July at these altitudes). Lupine and Indian paintbrush come in summer, which usually occurs in August. The red autumn leaves of mountain blueberries give the slopes color in fall.

The last half mile or so of the trail goes up over the eastern flank of Mount Ararat, providing wide views of Mt. Rainier and the park-like surroundings. Then it descends into the Hunting Ground, a complex of meadows, alpine forest and little lakes and tarns, where it intersects the Wonderland Trail (Hike 125). Turn to the right here and the Wonderland Trail will take you through meadows and then down the valley of Devil's Dream Creek. In a little less than a mile you'll reach Squaw Lake, set in a small meadow beneath forested slopes.

A more scenic side trip is available if you turn left at the intersection and take the Wonderland Trail to another junction, about a quarter of a mile to the west. The Mirror Lakes Trail leads gently up slope towards the mountain through meadows and woods. In 0.6 miles the trail reaches the tiny (but famous) Mirror Lakes (Hike 114).

Indian Henry's formerly was the usual first overnight stop on the Wonderland Trail for hikers going clockwise around the mountain. There was a ranger's cabin here and a log shelter for hikers. Overuse and trampled meadows brought an end to the camping and now through hikers stay at Devil's Dream Camp, two miles to the east, or Pyramid Creek Camp, further east yet.

For the clockwise Wonderland Trail hikers, the view of the mountain from Indian Henry's Hunting Ground is the first grand view, the one that makes the back-breaking heavy packs and sore feet worth it. Hikers up from Kautz Creek can get the same inspiring views in just a day.

Mt. Rainier is surrounded by an envelope of lowland forest of incomparable beauty. In the Northwest, where virgin forest is becoming alarmingly rare, an undisturbed example of the great conifers and their understory companions is hard to find. Almost 150 years of logging and clearing have reduced them to farms, malls, housing developments and tame second growth woods. Mt. Rainier National Park, established in 1901, was saved from the loggers early enough to provide a splendid example of what the great Northwest forests once were like. Here is a wonderful, short trail trip through a particularly beautiful section of this forest.

The Twin Firs Trail is not well known and is absent from most guide books and maps, yet it is right there on the busy road between the Park entrance and Longmire. There is no obvious trailhead sign, so users must be on the lookout for it, guided by the mileage. When your odometer nears 4 miles past the Nisqually Entrance Station, watch for a pullout on the left where the road is curving to the right. It's the correct one if you see a low display sign mounted at the foot of the forest rise. Park here and read the sign, which describes the various trees of the lowland forest. Above the road is the Twin Firs Trail, consisting of a 0.4 mile loop trip. (In 2005 the sign was missing, though the stone pillar of its mounting was there).

About 100 yards into the forest the trail nears the first of some really giant Douglas Firs. This one is many hundreds of years old and a couple of hundred feet tall. It was a mature tree when Columbus arrived in the New World.

The primary trees of this forest are three: Douglas Firs, Western Hemlock and Western Red Cedar. All three grow to prodigious size if given the chance. Under them, where the sun rarely shines (even when the sky is clear) the vegetation consists mostly of shade-lovers: salal, sword ferns, twin flowers, bunchberry, trillium and Vine Maple trees.

The trail starts out gently and level, and then begins uphill, passing more giant Douglas Firs. Near the top it crosses a busy creek on a nicely-crafted bridge, one of three that cross the streams encountered. After a bit of high wandering, the route heads down again and eventually reaches the road a hundred yards or so west of the starting point.

Hike 4 – The Trail of the Shadows

map pg.25

The first trail taken by many visitors to Mt. Rainier is the inviting short nature trail at Longmire. Beginning just across the road from the Longmire village, the trail is rich in scenery, nature study and history. An informative booklet is usually available at the trailhead (if not, ask at the visitor center). It is a pleasant, gentle loop trip, suitable for children.

To start, cross the road from the village and turn right to begin the loop. The guide and most walkers take the loop in a counterclockwise direction. The trail winds around Longmire Meadow, a large grassy area that provides a nice view of the mountain above.The noise of the traffic, already quiet by city or highway standards, is soon lost and the quiet of the meadow and the deep forest gives a pleasant feeling of remoteness.

If you are new to northwest trees, the markers will help you identify some of the more common trees of the Park: Douglas Fir, Western Hemlock and Western Red Cedar. Deer are frequent visitors to Longmire Meadow and you may even have a chance to glimpse a beaver or, at least, its architectural accomplishments. A beaver pond is visible from the trail a little way from the start.

The area was first developed because of its hot springs. The first example is encountered to the right of the trail, where a stone path leads to a spring; this one, however, is not at present an active hot spring.

Although the trail abounds in the shadows of its name, there are also patches of open forest, where tree growth has been affected by the unusual concentrations of minerals in the soil. Deep in the shadows about a quarter of a mile along the loop is a log cabin built by Elcain Longmire in 1888, when he was developing the area as a hot springs resort. Nearby is the remains of a bathing pool fed by the hot spring called "Iron Mike". The colorful water, rich in iron and other minerals, flows through the structure and continues down into the meadow.

Near the end of the loop there's a short spur down to a view of the rather disappointing "travertine mound", once a much bigger spectacle formed by a spring that built up a rusty-red heap of precipitates. Then the trail turns left at a junction and returns through trees to Longmire.

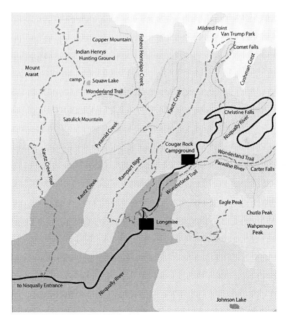

Map 3 Longmire North

Many years ago there were several campgrounds located at strategic places in Mt. Rainier National Park. As crowds grew in size and campers grew in their propensity to trample meadows and cut down trees for firewood, some of these campgrounds were seen to be serious sources of degradation of parkland. The campgrounds located in flowery meadows at Paradise and Sunrise were closed some 30 years ago and the large one at Longmire, once the chief campground in the park, was also closed. In place of these a new campground was opened at Cougar Rock, part way between Longmire and Paradise. The location makes excellent sense; it is set in a flat, wooded area with attractive near-private campsites, but away from major viewpoints or sensitive environments. The Park Service built new facilities for both the campground and the adjacent picnic area, even including special tables for the use of handicapped visitors.

Hikers can reach Cougar Rock from Longmire by using the Wonderland Trail. It is a pleasant trip, only 2 miles in length each way, passing through deep virgin forest never far from the Nisqually River. The elevation gain is minimal, only about 400 feet.

The hike makes a good mid-day trip if you bring a lunch to eat in the unusually attractive picnic area at Cougar Rock, which is on the east side of the Paradise Road. The campground is on the west side.

The Rampart Ridge Loop is a popular round trip hike from Longmire. Totaling 4.8 miles in length, the trail takes the hiker up onto the Ramparts and back again, with excellent views of Longmire and the Nisqually Valley from a viewpoint near mid-trail. The "ramparts" of this trail are the vertical cliffs formed long ago by the Nisqually Glacier when it extended down to the lowlands. The ice cut through the volcanic rock, sheering it off and carrying the rocky debris away downhill, leaving a wide U-shaped valley.

The loop can be followed in either direction. This description goes counterclockwise, which has the slight advantage of being a little less steep on the uphill part than the downhill. But either way is fine. Begin at the Longmire Information Center, where the trail sign can be found to the left of the building. The trail goes uphill at the right of the Paradise Road about 0.2 miles and then crosses the road. This part of the trip is on the Wonderland Trail, which is well marked with signs. The trail swings to the right and ascends slowly at first along the side of a hill that separates the trail from the road and the river. The forest is cool and deep.

There are no views for a while, as there are hills on both sides of trail. About a half mile past the road crossing the trail begins to go up more in earnest, with nine or ten switchbacks carrying you to the top of the ridge. A trail to the right goes to van Trump Park and farther points (Hike 8). Another trail junction comes about 0.2 miles farther,

where the Rampart Ridge Trail leaves the Wonderland Trail. Taking a right here will lead you to Indian Henry's Hunting Ground (Hike 7), a little under 5 miles from here. The Rampart Ridge Trail goes left, ascending gradually along the backbone of the ridge through pleasant forest.

A little over a mile from the trail junction there is a short spur trail that leads to an excellent viewpoint. Mt. Rainier, Longmire and the Nisqually Valley are visible to the north and east. Directly east is the sharp summit of Eagle Peak.

It's all downhill from here. Switchbacks take you from the ridge summit at 4100 feet to Longmire at 2700 feet. Just before it reaches Longmire, the trail joins the Trail of the Shadows (Hike 4) for its final 0.1 mile.

Indian Henry's Hunting Ground, one of Rainier's premier alpine parks, can be reached from three directions via three different trails. The shortest route is along the Kautz Creek (Hike 2), but the approach from Longmire via Rampart Ridge is perhaps the most popular one, as it follows the Wonderland Trail (Hike 125). For a day hike it's a long one, 12.5 miles round trip. But the destination is worth the effort. Backpackers can make it a two or three day outing if they reserve a space at the camps at Devil's Dream or Pyramid Creek.

The trip begins at Longmire. Look for the Wonderland Trail sign just west of the Longmire Wilderness Information Center.

The initial 1.8 miles are described in the Rampart Ridge Loop section (Hike 6). They consist of forest travel, including some steep switchbacking over Rampart Ridge. The trail tops the ridge and makes a quick descent into the Kautz Creek Valley. This creek has a history of devastating flooding (see Hike 1) and it has not been easy for the Park Service to keep a footbridge here. Short switchbacks down to the creek will bring you to the latest version of this crossing.

From the bridge the trail crosses the rather flat central valley formed long ago by the Kautz Glacier. Perched in the forest of this valley is small Pyramid Creek Camp. A few hundred feet farther on, the trail crosses Pyramid Creek, a fairly vigorous stream that has its headwaters above in the seldom visited Pyramid Park and the scrappy Pyramid Glaciers. The trail then turns north to follow the valley of Fishers Hornpipe Creek, which it crosses after a few switchbacks. The next half mile or so is spent traversing along the lower south slopes of Iron Mountain and then it reaches another camp, the somewhat larger Devil's Dream Camp. Not far beyond is a small flowery meadow.

The trail is now above 5000 feet and the country is more alpine in nature. Views begin to open up and glimpses of the mountain are possible. Squaw Lake, about a quarter mile beyond the Camp, is a good-sized subalpine pond.

The trail next crosses Devil's Dream Creek. This creek with its inscrutable name is both the source and the outlet of Squaw Lake. Upper Devil's Dream Creek comes down from Indian Henry's to the west and lower Devil's Dream Creek leaves the lake near the inlet, to carry the waters down to meet Pyramid Creek.

A half mile or so beyond Squaw Lake

28

the trail enters Indian Henry's Hunting Ground. It is not a flat parkland like Yakima Park (Chapter 8) or Grand Park (Hike 80), but rather a rolling countryside with knolls and copses and fields and hillsides of flowers.

A crossroads is reached at mileage 6.3, where the Kautz Creek Trail (Hike 2) takes off to the left. Following the Wonderland Trail a little farther brings you to another crossroads, with the Mirror Lakes Trail (Hike 114) taking off to the right. Both trails allow more exploration of this large complex of alpine wonders, with all of the time the rugged western cliffs of Mt. Rainier rising above to the northeast.

There are two ways to hike to the flower fields of Van Trump Park. The trail via Rampart Ridge is the less used; it is longer and is in forest most of the way. Hikers seeking solitude should choose it, as the other route, via Comet Falls, is busy, especially on a sunny summer weekend. Another reason for choosing the Rampart Ridge route might be that the trail starts at Longmire and hikers based there might find it more convenient than having to drive or find a ride up the Paradise Road to the Comet Falls trailhead.

The one way distance from Longmire to Van Trump Park is 4.5 miles. The first four of these miles is spent in deep forest. The trail is excellent and the forest splendid, with a sequence of characteristics that change as elevation is gained. From the Douglas Fir of the low forest at Longmire, the trees change to a population that includes Western Hemlock, and then gradually the higher elevation trees take over: Pacific Silver Fir, Alaska Cedar and Subalpine Fir.

To begin, take the Wonderland Trail from Longmire. Either start in Longmire itself where the trail sign is found just west of the Longmire Hikers' Center or drive up the Paradise Road a short distance and park in a small parking area on the right, from which you can cross the road to the Wonderland Trail sign. The forest trail ascends first gradually and then steeply to the top of Rampart Ridge.

A trail junction on Rampart Ridge is reached in about 1.6 miles. Go to the right. From this point on the trail stays near the top of the ridge, providing an easy, gradual ascent towards the mountain. Fleeting glimpses of the outer world do occasionally occur, but it's mostly forest. After about 4 miles the trail begins a steep ascent of a ridge, with several switchbacks. This is a signal telling you that you are near the glories of some high alpine parkland.

Just as it breaks out of the woods into a narrow open valley, the trail comes to a junction. To the right is the trail to Van Trump Park proper and to the left is a trail to a spectacular high knoll called Mildred Point (Hike 14). Taking the right branch, you descend into the flower-filled realm of Van Trump Creek (its west fork) and then climb up to the main park, with its clumps of subalpine trees and lush meadows. The more popular route to this alpine park is via Comet Falls (Hike 13). Even on a weekend you may not encounter any other hikers on the way to Van Trump Park, but it's likely that there will be people there, having taken the shorter route.

As you rest against a log and gaze at the mountain, you might wonder just who was this Van Trump, anyway? His name is on the parkland, on the creek in the valley and on the cluster of glaciers that feed the creek.

Philemon B. Van Trump, born in Ohio, had come to Washington Territory in 1867 to serve as private secretary to Governor Marshall Moore. While residing in Olympia he became enamored with the mountain that rose so conspicuously above the other Cascades. Teaming up with two other men, Hazard Stevens and Edmund Coleman, who had similar ideas, he arranged to climb the mountain, which purportedly had not been climbed at that time. The three set out with a Yakima Indian guide named Sluiskin in August of 1870. Coleman soon dropped out, but Van Trump and Stevens, against Sluiskin's exhortations regarding the dangers of such an attempt, left the guide near Paradise Valley and eventually reached the summit, where they were forced to spend the night in a fumarole's cave in the summit crater. Thus the Van Trump features of Rainier are named for one of its first two "conquerors".

Hazard Stevens has not been ignored; his name graces an important canyon, as well as a mountain peak, a creek, a ridge and a glacier, all east of the Paradise region.

High above Van Trump Park one can see a feature named for another Indian Guide, a member of the Nisqually tribe named Wapowety. He was the guide for a party of adventurers from Fort Steilacoom led by Lieutenant A. V. Kautz. In 1857 the five men made the first recorded attempt to climb the mountain. In spite of a lack of equipment, lack of adequate clothing, lack of food and lack of time, Kautz was not turned back until reaching an altitude that was only a few hundred feet below the top.

Wapowety Cleaver is a sharp rocky feature separating the Van Trump Glaciers from Kautz Glacier. It is near the center of the mountain as seen from Van Trump Park.

The Eagle Peak trail provides one of those trips that has many pleasant features but then, at the very end, gives you a whopper. The trail spends almost all of its time on the south slopes of the mountain named Eagle Peak, but then, as it finally reaches its end, it opens up the view to the north with Mt. Rainier in one of its most spectacular visages.

The trail is moderate in most ways, moderate in length (3.5 miles), moderately strenuous in elevation gained (just under 3000 feet) and moderately varied, with much deep forest, some open, if fairly vertical, meadowland and many fine views. It is easy to reach, being right near the Hiking Center at Longmire. Find the trailhead across the bridge over the Nisqually, on the left a couple of hundred feet from the bridge.

The trail actually goes to a saddle between the summit of Eagle Peak and the next Tatoosh Range peak to the east, Chutla Peak. This saddle provides a marvelous view and it is not necessary to go farther, which the trail wisely does not do. However, if you have mountaineering skill, it is possible to follow a climbers' scramble route an additional half mile to Eagle's top.

The first three miles out of Longmire are in forest. There are occasional windows of sunlight and glimpses out at the world as the trail switchbacks steadily upward. For the first two miles it stays fairly close to an unnamed stream that lies in its valley on the left. Then it crosses the stream and switchbacks to the north and east. At three miles the forest opens up and views to the south and east provide inspiration to continue on to increasingly wider views.

The last half mile is a steep but exhilarating meadow hike, with the rugged, rocky Tatoosh peaks lining the eastern horizon. The more open view to the south includes several clearcuts in the adjacent national forest and, in the distance, the blunt, abbreviated summit Mt. St. Helens. Switchbacks in the steep meadow carry the hiker past spring grasses, alpine flowers and low mountain blueberries, each fragrant according to the season.

Finally the saddle is reached and the spectacle of Rainier is spread out before you. Unlike the foreshortened views from Paradise, this view includes the whole mountain, from the depths of the Nisqually valley below to the very summit at Columbia Crest, nearly 9000 feet above you.

To the west is the blocky, rocky summit of Eagle Peak, just a few feet less than 6000 feet above sea level. Turn right to view the spires of the Tatooshes: Chutla, Lane and Pinnacle. And turn around to see majestic Mt. Adams to the southeast.

A trip on the Wonderland Trail to Carter Falls is one of the nicest intermediate altitude short trips in the park. In early summer when the Paradise trails are still buried in snow, this trail is often open and inviting. One can reach the falls by taking the Wonderland Trail from Longmire, but the more common plan is to hike from either the Cougar Rock Campground or the nearby point where the Wonderland Trail encounters the Paradise Road. From this intersection Carter Falls is 1.1 miles east on the trail. Hikers starting in the Campground will add a quarter mile to that.

From the small parking area on the Paradise Road the trail immediately descends to the Nisqually River, which it crosses on a series of log bridges. Depending on what the river has been doing, there are usually two bridges that cross two main water channels. A glacial stream like the Nisqually can be unpredictable in spring and at times of flooding, so these bridges are sometimes a little temporary. At any time they can seem somewhat adventurous to use, as they bounce under your feet a little above the turbulent waters. While on the bridge, take a moment to tear your eyes away from the rapids beneath you to look to the left, upriver, at the mountain. This will be your only view of it on this trip, which remains sequestered in the Paradise River valley from here on.

Part of the way between the bridges and the falls is on a broad, nearly level trail that used to be a service road. Water pipes and electrical cables intrude upon the wilderness feeling, but the attractiveness of the surrounding forest is compensation. The trail follows the relatively quiet Paradise River. This stream is quite a contrast to the turbulent Nisqually, which has as its source the massive Nisqually Glacier. That river's water is a whitish grey color, caused by the large amount of fine rock dust (called "glacial flour")

that is formed as the giant sheet of ice grinds its way down its valley. The Paradise River, on the other hand, is formed in Paradise Valley, mostly from snow melt, and is clear and clean.

The first waterfall to be encountered is Carter Falls, a cataract about 50 feet high in the Paradise River. From the trail it is seen from above through the lacy branches of hemlocks and huckleberries. The falls were named after Harry Carter, who built much of this trail up to Paradise in the late 19th century.

But don't stop here. Nature has provided a bonus falls just a short distance farther up the trail, where the river tumbles over Madcap Falls, a different style of cataract in which the water cascades down in a series of leaps over the rocks.

Hikers camping at Cougar Rock who have more time than it takes to get to Carter Falls should consider going farther up the Wonderland Trail, visiting more waterfalls. The trip from the campground to Narada Falls, a worthy goal, is almost exactly 3 miles. The trail is not very steep and the forest, the accompanying Paradise River, and the occasional views are all superb.

The portion of the trail to Carter Falls is described in Hike 10. The Wonderland Trail continues gradually up the valley, passing the ruins of an old wire-wrapped wooden water pipe on the right. Next the trail crosses over the river to begin an ascent of the east side of the valley. Soon it reaches a trail junction. The branch to the left continues up the valley to Narada Falls, about 0.3 miles farther on. The trail to the right is the continuation of the Wonderland Trail, which leaves the Paradise River valley to head south and then east to the Reflection Lakes (see Hike 29).

The Narada Falls are one of the most spectacular falls of the park. Also, they are probably the most visited, as the Paradise Road passes directly by them and there is a large parking lot and resulting crowds, all at the top of the falls. The trail from below arrives at the bottom of the falls and gets an excellent view of them, far better than what is seen by the folks above, many of whom do not choose to get more than 50 feet from their cars.

The Falls were named by members of the Theosophical Society more than 100 years ago after the Hindu word for "pure". The Paradise River does appear pure, especially when compared to more glacier-contaminated rivers like the Nisqually. The drop, counting both horsetail and plunge, is 240 feet, making it one of the taller falls of Mt. Rainier, though not as tall as Comet Falls' 320 foot plunge (Hike 12).

Mt. Rainier has many beautiful waterfalls. One of the tallest and most famous is 320-foot high Comet Falls. The hike to the falls is a scenic one, not too long (only 1.9 miles each way) for a pleasant half-day's outing. The trailhead is located about 10½ miles up the Paradise Road from Longmire. There is limited parking, so get there early if it's a weekend. The trailhead is well marked with a large sign and a map of the trail.

The route begins fairly steeply and in a short time crosses Van Trump Creek on a handsome, sturdy log bridge. The trail will stay fairly close to this creek for the entire trip and its cheerful sound will provide frequent background music for the hike. The trail is mostly through forest, but there are several open spots along the way. One of them allows a nice view of the top of Rainier. There is a broad talus slope that gives the hiker a view both up the hillside and down towards the creek.

Next comes a steep portion of trail when it switchbacks up a forested slope populated mostly by Western Hemlocks. Then it levels off and passes under a columnar cliff and through another talus slope. Small creeks tumble down from the right, one of which has a small waterfall. Soon a larger creek is encountered. This is actually one of the two branches of Van Trump Creek. The confluence of the two creek branches is to the left. The trail crosses over the east branch, which comes down from the right.

Beyond the bridge, the trail climbs the slope to the north and then switchbacks up steeply to the base of Comet Falls. A short side trail leads close to the falls, where you can feel the mist, hear the roar and drink in one the most glorious views of the region.

Both because it is shorter and enjoys more views, this is the more popular of the two trails to Van Trump Park. The trail is a continuation of the Comet Falls Trail (Hike 12), which has its trailhead off of the Paradise Road between Longmire and Paradise. For the first part of the trail see Hike 12.

Beyond Comet Falls the trail ascends steeply up a woodsy and grassy slope to the right of the falls. Many switchbacks lead towards the alpine parkland and the trail crosses several small streams along the way. Looking back from an open area one can see the southern mountains spread out in the distance, with the truncated cone of Mt. St. Helens dimly visible as a western outpost of the range, while Mt. Adams' snowy dome marks the eastern edge of Washington's south Cascades.

The high point of the trail is at about 5500 feet, where the meadows, rolling hills and clumps of subarctic trees make up the park and the view is dominated by Mt. Rainier. The meadows of Van Trump Park are a popular destination. In the "good old days" it was possible to camp here, making use of a traditional log shelter.

Overuse, a constant problem at Mt. Rainier, eventually brought an end to overnighting here. The shelter is now gone but the fields of flowers and the wonderful views remain.

The maintained trail ends at the meadows, except for a section that heads west, down into a small valley and thence up to Mildred Point (Hike 14). But an informal trail leads up towards the mountain. In late summer it is possible to follow the ridge up to where even better views are possible. For instance, to the east are the slopes of Cushman Crest.

Two Cushmans figure in Mt. Rainier's history. W. H. Cushman provided one of the United States flags carried to the summit by Stevens and Van Trump on their historic first ascent. This flag was somewhat historic itself, having been brought across the country 20 years earlier for the California gold rush. Because of its age it lacked 5 of the 37 stars that a contemporary flag should have had.

Cushman's flag wasn't the only unique flag carried to the summit by Stevens and Van Trump. The historical record shows another, this one made from material that General Stevens had prepared and given to one of the women, Fanny Yantis, who was accompanying the party on their approach toward the mountain. She forgot about the request that she sew the material into a flag until late on the Saturday before departure. Unable for religious reasons to work on the flag on Sunday, she and a friend, Lizzie Ferry, prepared the material and readied the needles and at midnight Sunday night began frantically to sew the flag together. By 6 AM it was done, but lacking time for a full compliment of stars, the women put on only 13. These were intended to represent the 13 original colonies, though they were put in a row instead of the original circle, making this flag a definite one-of-a-kind.

The second Cushman was State Representative Francis W. Cushman, who in 1903 pushed through the legislature an appropriation of $10,000 to finance the road to Paradise Valley.

Anyone who proceeds farther up Van Trump Ridge should remember the important rule of cross-country travel above timberline. Walk on snow or rocks; stay off the fragile high meadows, where plants have a terrible time surviving and can die if carelessly stepped on during their brief "summer" free of snow cover. If you must travel across an area of soil, use a well-established path rather than starting a new one, which will lead to a sad and ugly crisscross of wanton trails.

Proceeding carefully above Van Trump Park can bring you to views of sections of the Van Trump Glacier.

This glacier is made up of half a dozen individual fields of ice, spread out from near the top of Wapowety Cleaver at 9500 feet down to about 6500 feet above Cushman Crest.

Hikers who enjoy the high country should not miss the trail to Mildred Point. It provides the kind of distant views and rock and glacier close-ups that usually are reserved for off-trail climbers, and all are available from a well-maintained official trail.

Mildred Point can be reached from either Van Trump Park (Hike 13) or Rampart Ridge (Hike 8). It's only about a half mile from the Rampart Ridge Trail/Van Trump Park Trail junction to the end of the trail at the Point. The shortest route from the road is from the Comet Falls Trailhead (Hike 12), past the falls, up onto Van Trump Park and then south down to a creek crossing and the trail junction. From Longmire's Rampart Ridge Trailhead, it's a straight shot to Mildred Point on about 4 ½ miles of good trail.

From the junction the trail enters high meadowland, with clumps of subarctic trees here and there. Views begin to open up, with the Tatoosh Range dominating the southeastern horizon. As the trail steepens, the view back down to the south includes the nearby parkland, the Nisqually Valley, forested hills and the distant, misty summit of Mt. St. Helens. To the southeast the snow dome of Mt. Adams peeks out from behind a Tatoosh, with the Paradise Road conspicuous in the foreground, Ricksecker Point being visible at the right where the road curves away from view. And in the forward direction is the Mountain.

The trail ambles up to the top of a high knoll, which is Mildred Point.

The views from the top are superb. Rainier from here (in late summer) seems to be more rock than snow and ice. The foreground is bare slopes and cliffs of volcanic deposits. Lying on top of them is the Kautz Glacier, which reaches up nearly to the heights of Point Success. To the left and nestled above the Kautz is the Success Glacier, gathering snow and ice in its perch below the steep cliffs of Success Cleaver. To the east are Cushman Crest and the valley of Van Trump Creek. Directly below Mildred Point to the left is the snout of the Kautz Glacier and the awesome canyon of Kautz Creek.

Chapter 3 – The Paradise Region

The Paradise region is the most popular destination in the National Park. In fact, on a sunny weekend in the summer it can become so crowded with cars that there is no place for visitors to park and the Park Service has to close access to Paradise. Plans to solve the problem are being considered that are similar to those that have been used in other popular National Parks, such as Zion and Yosemite, where cars are left below near the Park entrance and buses carry visitors to the key destinations. At present these are still just plans and the crowding or closure can be frustrating. Wise visitors arrange to travel to Paradise on week days or in the autumn.

The name "Paradise" was first given to the beautiful meadows above the Nisqually by Virinda Longmire, who with her husband James Longmire, ran the first tourist hotel, located near the position of the present National Park Inn at Longmire (Chapter 2). It is sometimes speculated that if only she had named the area "Mosquito Flats", the problem of weekend crowding might not now be so acute.

The top of the Paradise Road is at an elevation of 5400 feet. The valleys and slopes here are snow-covered most of the year. Even in early summer there can be 20 feet of snow at Paradise and visitors must go through snow tunnels to enter the buildings. Usually by late July and until the first snows in October the Paradise region is clear of snow and the trails can be followed without skis or snowshoes. Although even then many visitors do not stray far from their cars, many cannot resist the temptations offered by the trail signs that are posted near the parking lots.

Facilities at Paradise include a wonderful old National Park-style hotel called Paradise Inn, open in summer and early fall. It is a historical gem and, although the rooms are simple and basic, the dining room is famous for its inspiring architecture and its food.

(Note: the Park Service has decided to close the Inn for two years, in 2006 and 2007, for structural work, but it is promised to re-open with all of its grand and historic features intact in 2008).

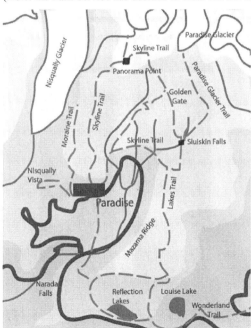

Other facilities include an ugly 1960's era Visitor Center, designed to look like a disheveled rocket ship, where there are excellent natural history displays and a source of relatively fast food. Plans have been announced for its eventual replacement. For climbers there is a guide hut where arrangements to climb the mountain can be made. There are now no camping facilities at Paradise, but there is a very attractive picnic area with tables and fabulous views of the Tatoosh Range.

Map 4 The Paradise Region

The two features that make Paradise so outstanding are its flowers and its glacier views. The flower fields extend from down in the valley below the Inn to the highest nearly bare rocks of the upper tundra. They are most luxurious at the level of the Paradise settlement, where a brief walk can take you to fields of avalanche lilies, Indian paintbrush, mountain asters, beargrass, squaw flowers, anemones, lupine and countless others. And only a short walk from the car can bring close-up views of glaciers, especially of the ice-jumbled Nisqually, which rises shimmering above the quiet meadows of Paradise.

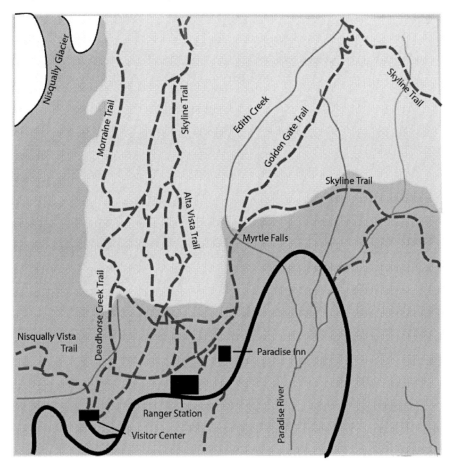

Map 5 Paradise

The two most popular trails in the Paradise area are the two "Vista Trails" that lead to Nisqually Vista and to Alta Vista. Both are short and paved and both can be taken as loop trails. Both start from the visitor center and both promise and deliver superb vistas.

The Nisqually Vista Trail is just a little more than a mile, roundtrip, and is about as level a trail as can be found in the Park. It leaves towards the mountain from the visitor center (or to the west from the other parking areas) and quickly turns left, crossing Dead Horse Creek in its miniature valley. Winding through some trees, it soon comes to a junction. Most people take the right-hand branch, which leads more directly to the vista. The left branch is what you return on.

About a half mile from the visitor center is one of this trail's highlights, a small lakelet called Fairy Pool, which provides a perfect reflection of the mountain. In fact, it is the view of this pond that is featured in the now-famous poster made during the WPA days. The silk-screen view of pool and mountain advertised the Ranger Naturalist Service of the Park for many years and copies of the poster are valuable collector's items. Like an up-side-down stamp, some of the value of this poster is caused by a mistake on the part of the artist, who showed the pond as a river. Instead, Fairy Pool is a gentle, shallow pond. This trail is, of course an excellent one for families with small children, who are usually fascinated by the pond and may sit down on a rock to stir the water.

In a little under a half mile the trail reaches the Vista, marked by a fence that rims the edge of a spectacular cliff. Stay back. The ground here is unstable, made up of loose glacial debris.

The view of the glacier is tremendous. Perched 900 feet above it, the Vista stop reveals a sweeping view of ice, extending from the gray, gravelly snout, with the infant Nisqually River issuing out from under the ice, to the high, serrated icefalls of the upper glacier. One of Rainier's longest glaciers, the Nisqually is a 4-mile long ribbon of ice. Its top is at Rainier's summit and the snout, visible from the Vista, is 9600 feet below the summit. Although the ice is slowly slipping down its precipitous valley (at an average rate of about 0.00001 miles per hour or a little less than an inch per hour), the glacier is melting at a slightly faster rate, so that the snout is moving slowly up the mountain. When the Park was created just over a hundred years ago, the glacier reached to where the Paradise road now crosses over the Nisqually River on its high bridge. The glacier has lost nearly a mile of length in that time.

Will it continue to shrink? Perhaps, but it also could turn around and start to grow again. Some glaciers in the Cascades have grown longer in recent years, though most are getting smaller. Glaciers are sensitive to subtle climate changes. As you continue on to complete the trail's loop and return to the visitor center, make plans to come back some time to check to see whether the glacier has grown. Any change will be seen clearly from Nisqually Vista.

Mt. Rainier is surrounded by hundreds of waterfalls, dozens of which are well-known enough to have been given official names. The most visited of them are both near Paradise: Narada Falls and Myrtle Falls. Both are an easy stroll from the car.

The trail trip to Myrtle Falls has the advantage of having wonderful views both of Rainier to the north and the opposite range, the Tatoosh Mountains, to the south. Also it passes through some of Paradise's most spectacular flower fields.

The trail begins at the parking lot and heads northeast, passing behind Paradise Inn. It's only a mile round trip to the falls and the trail is nearly level (and paved) all of the way. The views open up to the east of the Inn, especially to the south and east, with the Paradise Valley below and rising above it Mazama Ridge and the Tatoosh Range beyond. As the trail gently ascends it soon comes to some of those famous Paradise flowers.

About a half mile from the parking lot the trail dips to meet Edith Creek, which it crosses on a wooden bridge. Just below the bridge, visible from a short spur trail, is Myrtle Falls. The falls were named in 1909 by a mountain guide named Jules Stampfler, who named it after one of his clients. Unfortunately Myrtle's last name is lost to history.

The Alta Vista Trail is a little longer and rather steeper than the Nisqually Vista Trail, but seems to attract as many Paradise hikers. It provides a good workout and leg-stretching and the views from the trail and from the summit of the hill are well worth the effort. It is a loop trail a little more than a mile and a half in length, depending on the starting place. A total of 600 feet of elevation is gained and lost. The goal of the trail is the top of a mound that is wooded on its west side and open to the meadows above Edith Creek on its east side.

The main trailhead is behind the visitor center, where there is a map of area trails. An alternate start can be made from the eastern parking lot, where there is another sign. The trail is paved, not so much to protect your shoes, but more to protect the fragile meadows through which it travels. Always stay on the trails in this National Park, where the land is snow-covered most of the year. The meadow flowers and grasses have only a few weeks in order to grow and bloom and just one stomp by a boot can set them back years.

On the way up, the trail passes three trail junctions, the first a side trail from the east side parking lot, the second another side trail leading east and west, and the third the Skyline Trail leading north. A tenth of a mile past the Skyline Trail junction brings the hiker to the loop part of the trip. Staying right is the gentlest way up. The left branch is the usual way back down.

Another 0.2 miles brings the trail to a three way junction. The trail that takes off sharply to the left is the return trip, heading up to the top of Alta Vista. Just beyond this junction is the Skyline Trail again. The Alta Vista Trail goes up past a patch of trees to the high point, covered in high rocky meadowland with tundra-type flowers..

Hike 18 – The Dead Horse Creek Trail map pg. 46

The Dead Horse Creek Trail is included here because it's a named trail and has nice views, but does not have a specific destination (apparently the dead horse was carried off long ago). Its main purpose in life is to provide access from the Visitor Center to the Moraine Trail (Hike 19) and the Skyline Trail (Hike 20). The trail totals just about one mile in length, ending where it joins the Skyline Trail just below Glacier Vista. It follows Dead Horse Creek, a part-time water course, over most of its length.

The Moraine Trail is one of the least traveled trails in the Paradise region and can give a visitor a bit of respite from the crowds nearby. Its pluses include some up-close geology and some glorious views, both up at the mountain and down the deep valley of the Nisqually towards the south.

The trail's length is about a mile from Paradise, depending on where you park your car. The shortest way is to leave from the Visitor Center, taking the Dead Horse Creek Trail (Hike 18) about a half mile to the Moraine Trail trailhead. Alternate routes are possible from elsewhere among the vast parking lots at Paradise. Just keep left (heading west) at trail intersections.

The Moraine Trail sign points left from the Dead Horse Creek Trail, where there is a fine view of the mountain and the glacier. The trail takes off downhill, heads briefly southwest and then turns to the north to provide another mountain view. It passes through a grove of trees as it descends. Emerging from the woods, it enters a steep meadow, passes a pretty stream and then climbs up onto the rocky inner slopes of the moraine.

The moraine is like a wall of rock debris, made up of material brought down from above on the glacier's surface and deposited along the side of the ice as the glacier moved and melted. On the far side of this ridge of debris is the glacier and on the near side is the valley that was left as the glacier shrank from the time long ago when it filled this entire area. The Moraine Trail ascends the morainal ridge and ends at an elevation of about 5700 feet.

Notice the rocks here; they include a wide variety of sizes from huge boulders to fine sand grains. All of these rocks were ground from the sides of the valley by the ice and transported down piggyback from somewhere higher in the glacier's course.

Mt. Rainier has been carved and whittled away by its glaciers. It was once about 2000 feet higher than now. The ice rivers on its top and sides have reduced its height and torn away much of its sides. A good demonstration of the glacier's past action is found on the Wonderland Trail (Hike 125), which circumnavigates the mountain, with huge amounts of ups and downs from ridge tops to the many deep glacial valleys.

From the end of the trail there is a wonderful view of Rainier, rising 9000 feet above the glacier at your feet. In the opposite direction the view is also fine. Down the rock-strewn ice is the snout of the glacier and far below is the bridge. Only a hundred years ago the glacier's ice reached all the way down to near where the bridge is now.

The Skyline Trail is one of the premier trails in Mt. Rainier National Park. It's a loop trip with a total length of 5.2 miles. It makes a marvelous all-day hike, but it also can be done in a vigorous afternoon. All of the trail lies above timberline, so it's generous with alpine flowers, distant viewpoints and snow. In fact the snow is a problem until late summer, as it's under snow cover many years until late July. It's best to travel it in August or September.

The Skyline Trail begins in the Paradise parking lot near the ranger station, though any of the several trailheads at Paradise can eventually connect to it. To get the best views while hiking, it's usually traveled in a clockwise direction. Trail signs should be followed straight up towards the mountain from Paradise.

The Skyline Trail ascends fairly steeply, skirting around Alta Vista on the left. The tundra-like alpine meadows here are very fragile and the Park Service tries to keep hikers on the trail by placing rock-lined trail edges and reminder signs along the way.

For the first 1.7 miles the trail stays on the west side of the ridge, providing excellent views of the crevasses of the Nisqually Glacier far below. For the best views and an explanatory signboard, take the side trail left to Glacier Vista, a minimal detour that's well worth it. Above Glacier Vista the Skyline Trail no longer encounters even small patches of trees; its all volcanic rock and snow. At 6600 feet the trail switchbacks right and climbs along steep cliffs. Views to the south open up as the way proceeds on rock steps up the side of the ridge.

Panorama Point is 2 miles from the start and is an excellent place to stop and admire the views of the Tatoosh Range and the Cascades farther south. A Park Service sign helps to identify the various peaks that are in view and a rock monument marks the spot. On an exceptionally clear day it's possible to see not only Mt. Adams in southern Washington but also the white triangular peak of Mt. Hood in Oregon.

Down below, the trails above Paradise are laid out like a map. Alta Vista is on the right and the other end of the Skyline Trail is on the left, where the Golden Gate Trail can be seen joining it near Myrtle Creek. Looking the other way, the Skyline Trail is seen meandering its way up the ridge to its high point.

This is the "High" Skyline Trail branch. Another trail, the "Low" Skyline Trail leaves Panorama Point down to the east, but it is usually snow covered and often closed because of dangerous snow conditions. The high point of the High Trail is at 7050 feet, amid rocks and heather. From there the trail swings around to the east along the top of a valley and then descends fairly steeply to meet the Low branch's snowy realm.

The trail gently descends as it nears the Golden Gate and settles onto Mazama Ridge. At these more temperate altitudes, blue Lupine, Indian Paintbrush and Beargrass bloom in season.

Just under a mile from Panorama Point there's a trail junction at Golden Gate, which provides a shortcut back to Paradise for those in a hurry (Hike 22). But the Skyline Trail still has much to offer. Beyond the junction it gently descends on the top of the ridge through flower fields and meadowland.

About a half mile from Golden Gate the trail swings around to the north and drops into the valley of the infant Paradise River. Near a bridge there's a trail junction here with the Paradise Glacier Trail (Hike 23), which ascends the valley back north to the glacier, which formerly was famous for its giant ice caves. The route lies beneath the crumbly spire of Little Tahoma. As the Skyline Trail descends, views of Rainier and the eroded slopes of Mazama Ridge dominate the northern skyline and trees once again are encountered in their artistic alpine clumps. A half mile farther is another trail junction, this one with the Lakes Trail (Hike 26), which continues down on the top of the ridge to the Reflection Lakes. The Skyline Trail turns right to begin a spectacular descent to Paradise Valley.

Off to the west from the trail is the Paradise highway and Paradise Inn.The descent by switchbacks is rather steep but scenic. Near the bottom the trail follows along the bubbling baby Paradise River, here a series of waterfalls. The trail then contours to the west towards Paradise, crossing a sturdy bridge over another stream destined to become part of the Paradise River. Gaining height gradually, the trail comes to its last creek crossing, this one of Edith Creek (Hike 16).

The final stretch of trail heads toward Paradise Inn and the acres of cars at Paradise.

The Pebble Creek Trail is a short (about 2/3 mile) extension of the Skyline Trail (Hike 20) up towards Camp Muir (Hike 24). It leaves the Skyline Trail where it is traversing the slope below Panorama Point and proceeds directly north towards the mountain. The official trail ends at about 7300 feet, where the route up encounters a permanent snow field. During much of the summer, of course, hikers will encounter semi-permanent snow fields down closer to Paradise, depending on the rate of snow melt in a particular year. About half way up there is a short spur trail that leads to the right to the High Skyline Trail.

The Pebble Creek Trail crosses its namesake near the end, where the creek tumbles down from snowfields to finally end far below in the Nisqually Glacier.

The Golden Gate is a notch in the ridge high above the north end of Paradise Valley. The trail to it runs straight up from Paradise. The trailhead is about 0.6 miles from the parking area (depending on where you park). It branches off from the Skyline Trail a little ways past the bridge over Edith Creek and Myrtle Falls. From there it starts up, first gradually and then more steeply, using switchbacks to make the ascent comfortably. The slope is open to the south and in summer it is ablaze with flowers.

These slopes are also excellent places for watching marmots warming themselves in the summer sun or gathering food to store in their rock homes for the winter.

At the top of the switchbacks the trail passes through a small stand of trees and just a mile from the start it reaches the top of the ridge, where views are spectacular. There it intersects the Skyline Trail (Hike 20) and hikers can, if they wish, make a loop trip of it by going either direction from here. To the left the way ascends to the barren alpine heights before circling around to Paradise. To the right the trail descends gradually along the scenic top of the ridge, finally intersecting the Lakes Trail (Hike 26) before descending into Paradise Valley.

It is common to use the Golden Gate Trail in the opposite way, to form a loop with the Skyline Trail, descending on the Golden Gate, which is somewhat more appealing going down than up. And the views on the descent are wonderful.

Historically the Paradise Glacier Trail was constructed to take visitors to an amazing phenomenon, one that no longer exists. In the first half of the last century the bottom of the Paradise Glacier was the location of some wonderful ice caves, carved from the ice of this nearly stagnant glacier by meltwater streams. Famous photographs of the era show large rooms below the ice, bathed in the deep blue color of the interior light. Some show the cave entrance framing the distant peak of Mt. Adams.

Some of the ice is still there and Mt. Adams is still in the distance, but the caves are now gone. The main reason for taking the trail now is for the grand views, the high tundra habitat, extreme flowers and a chance to get up close to a glacier without falling into a crevasse.

The trail leaves the Skyline Trail about a half mile below the Golden Gate, a little south of the crossing of the two creeks that inhabit the upper Paradise Valley. The intersection is near the Stevens-Van Trump Historical Monument, located approximately where the two who first climbed Rainier, Isaac Stevens and Philomen Van Trump, left their Indian Guide, Sluiskin, to begin their climb.

The trail is 1.4 miles long. It gains 400 feet in elevation from the trail intersection, peaking at 6400 feet near the glacier. Leaving the Skyline Trail, it turns abruptly north and traverses up a broad plateau. The views open up as altitude is gained and flowers line the path in season.

On the way to the glacier the trail passes some permanent ice fields, remnants of the lower Paradise Glacier of 100 years ago. Old maps show that the upper half of the present trail was under the deep ice of the glacier in the late 1890's. Where you now walk among polished rocks and dry creek beds, not long ago there was a thick sheet of crevassed ice with underground streams connecting large icy caverns. Tourists armed with lanterns and ice axes once roamed among the caves.

The present terminus of the glacier is merely a stream issuing from the melting snow and ice. This photograph, taken 50 years ago, shows the shallow caves that remained at that time.

It is an interesting experience to get so near to a glacier. However, only skilled and well-equipped mountaineers should venture out onto the surface of even this relatively even-tempered ice sheet.

Hike 24 – Camp Muir

The trip to Camp Muir can be a tremendous thrill, but it also can be a tragedy. The destination is a group of alpine huts at an altitude of 10,188 ft., high above timberline and perched among rocks and glaciers. In good weather it is possible to reach the site safely, but if clouds move in, as they often do, the route can become treacherous, as cliffs and crevasses threaten on either side. An experienced hiker, equipped with an ice axe and the knowledge of how to use it and with navigation equipment and navigating skills, should be able to reach Camp Muir without much trouble. Trouble can happen, though, when, for instance, a sudden summer snowstorm descends without warning. A surprising number of people have been killed between Paradise and Camp Muir. McClure Rock, which is passed on this route, provides an historical example. It memorializes the mountain's first climbing tragedy, when Prof. Edgar McClure of the University of Oregon fell to his death from this rock while leading a descent from the summit, where he had made measurements with a barometer to determine the height of the mountain.

During most of the summer most of the trip is on snow. Heavy, waterproof boots, an ice axe and the ten essentials should be on your feet, in your hands and in your pack.

The distance to Camp Muir is 4.3 miles and the elevation gain is close to 4800 feet. The route follows the Skyline Trail (Hike 20) towards Panorama Point, but branches off to the left below the point, following the Pebble Creek Trail (Hike 21). Soon the way is all snow and the view to the Tatoosh Mountains is downwards.

The route is near the crest of the Muir Icefield, a generally crevasse-free expanse of permanent snow that blankets the ridge between the Paradise and Cowlitz Glaciers on the east and the Nisqually Glacier on the west. The snow is blindingly white on sunny days. Be sure to apply sun screen and wear dark glasses.

Camp Muir is nestled on a small flat space at the bottom of Cowlitz Cleaver. There are rough stone buildings, often crowded with summiters, both coming and going.

Hike 25 – The Sluiskin Falls Loop map pg. 45

Hikers with only a limited time at Paradise, but who want to have a high country adventure can take the Sluiskin Falls Loop trip, made up of sections of the Skyline Trail (Hike 20) combined with the Golden Gate Trail (Hike 22). One can go either way on this loop, which is a total of 3.3 miles in length. Going counterclockwise gives the best views and the Golden Gate Trail is really more pleasant going down than up.

Starting at the Paradise ranger station, one takes the Skyline Trail past Myrtle Falls and then down hill gently into the lower Paradise Valley. After crossing the infant Paradise River on a footbridge, the hiker faces an uphill stretch, with switchbacks, to gain the top of Mazama Ridge. At the top of the climb, the trail levels off onto a plateau, where it encounters the intersection with the Lakes Trail.

The route then swings around to head north and up to reach the 6000 foot elevation near the top of Sluiskin Falls, which is a nice, picturesque waterfall that most people never notice, as, ironically, it's not visible from any convenient vantage point on the Sluiskin Falls loop trip, though they can be seen in the distance from Paradise. The falls can just be made out near the top center of this view taken from the trail about 1/3 mile past the trailhead.

The falls are named for the Indian guide who accompanied Stevens and van Trump when they made the first climb of the mountain in 1870. Sluiskin waited apprehensively for the climbers in the meadows near here. There is a stone monument next to the trail near where Sluiskin waited, commemorating the first climb of the mountain and the patience of the guide who stayed behind. It was erected in 1921 by the Seattle Mountaineers and the Portland Mazamas.

Past the Monument and the narrow Upper Paradise Valley, the trail heads towards the Golden Gate with excellent Rainier views most of the way. Turn left at Golden Gate and head steeply down. Regain the Skyline Trail one mile below the Gate, near the bridge crossing Edith Creek. From here it's just 0.3 miles back to the ranger station.

A beautiful and popular area near Paradise is the flat valley that houses the four Reflection Lakes. The main Reflection Lake is one of the park's three largest lakes (the other two are Louise Lake, a half mile to the east, and Mowich Lake in the northwest corner of the park). Most people who visit the Reflection Lakes do so by car, as they are a short three miles from Paradise on the Stevens Canyon Road. A more enjoyable way to visit them is provided by a scenic loop trail from Paradise that makes an easy 4.5 mile day hike through varied and enchanting meadows and woods.

The loop trail can be taken in either direction, of course, and can be started either at Paradise or at Reflection Lakes. The following description takes it from Paradise counterclockwise. In this direction one gets a long glorious period of looking directly at Rainier while hiking the return leg along the meadows of Mazama Ridge.

The Paradise trailhead is rather inconspicuously located at the southern end of the parking lot next to the Paradise Inn. The trail drops abruptly from the busy sea of cars and is soon out of sight and sound of the tourist hordes. As it descends into lower Paradise Valley, subalpine woods are to the left and the meadows to the right have the peculiar name of "Barn Flats". Presumably in the days when tourists came here by horse there was a horse barn in the region. In a little less than a half mile the trail arrives at the end of the valley. Lower Paradise valley is a flat, open grassy valley that provides great views up towards the mountain, Paradise Inn and, occasionally, bears.

At the bottom of the valley the trail reaches a junction with a trail to Narada Falls (Hike 29). This is an enchanting area with views of the waterfalls formed as the little river begins its drop from the valley down towards the Nisqually. The trail crosses the river on a picturesque foot bridge and then begins an uphill section that takes it first across the Paradise Valley Road and then up into the dense forest of lower Mazama Ridge. Near the top of the ridge there is an opening to give a view back of the mountain, but this section of trail is mostly through cool forest.

Beyond the crest the trail comes to an intersection with the High Lakes Trail (Hike 27) and later passes through some open meadowland. A mile and a half from Paradise is the junction with the Wonderland Trail and the first views of the Reflection Lakes.

The route goes left on the Wonderland Trail, passing the lakes between them and the parking areas, which are usually full of cars on sunny days. About half way along the main Reflection Lake the trail gives up and goes up to join the road for a quarter mile before once again becoming a trail. Watch for the roadside trail sign. The trail north from the road passes through an area of huckleberry bushes and along the marshy banks of Little Reflection Lake. There are four reflection lakes. Beyond Little Reflection Lake to the northwest is Littler Reflection Lake and hidden by a forested mound is Littlest Reflection Lake (these are not official names).

A few hundred yards from the road the Lakes Trail leaves the Wonderland Trail, which turns off to the right to descend to Louise Lake. The Lakes Trail heads north and up through a mixture of huckleberry meadows and scattered woods, with views back to the peaks of the Tatooshes.

In the autumn this area is a wonderland of berry bushes. The brilliant red leaves of the huckleberries and mountain blueberries are accompanied, on a warm day, by the smell of berries cooking in the sun, like a blueberry pie in the oven.

The trail reaches a high point when it comes to a rocky prominence called Faraway Rock. The views out to the Tatoosh Range are superb and directly below the rock, seemingly straight down the cliff, is blue Louise Lake.

A few steps farther up the trail is gem-like Faraway Lake, perched on a shelf above Stevens Canyon. As the trail ascends, the views to the east are remarkable. Stevens Canyon lies below the wall-like Stevens Ridge. Turning to the southeast brings another memorial to General Stevens into view, Stevens Peak, the easternmost of the Tatoosh Range peaks.

Just short of a mile from Reflection Lakes is a trail junction. The trail to the left is the High Lakes Trail, a scenic route that forms a nice loop trip from the lakes (Hike 27). The main Lakes Trail continues straight north and skirts along a fresh circular meadow (freshly meadowed; not too many years ago it was a pond, now filled in).

The views to the south open further, showing more and more of the Tatoosh peaks, including The Castle and Pinnacle and Plummer Peaks. Ahead Rainier rises above the northern horizon. From here on it dominates the hiker's vision. The country becomes a nearly flat open meadow with creek beds scattered across it and patches of sualpine trees here and there.

These meadows are home to flowers and berries that change with the seasons. At the height of the flower season, usually in late July, the high meadows are a medley of paintbrush, lupine, mountain daisies and valerian.

At a distance of two miles from the Reflection Lakes the Lakes Trail ends and the rest of the trip is made on the Skyline Trail, which comes down from the right and heads left over the edge of the ridge towards Paradise, 1.3 miles away to the west.

Chapter 4 – The Stevens Canyon Region

Stevens Canyon, southeast of Paradise, is traversed by the Stevens Canyon Road, which connects Paradise, Longmire and points west with the Ohanapecosh River area. The road is open only in the summer, as it is snow covered much of the year. Most of the trailheads are near the west end at Reflection Lakes, though there are a few farther east.

The road itself is a remarkable engineering feat that has defaced the canyon irreparably, though most park visitors are willing to ignore its ugly scars in order to have the opportunity to range across the park in cars. Many tourists (and tourist busses) take this road as part of a "round the mountain" trip that skirts the south and east sides of the park.

Cars tend to bunch up at two locations along the road, at the Reflection Lakes and at Box Canyon. There is a parking area and there are several trailheads at the lakes and more complete tourist facilities (picnic areas, restrooms and more trailheads) can be found at Box Canyon.

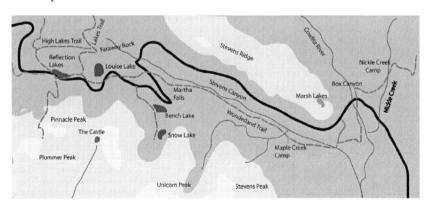

Map 6 Stevens Canyon West

Hikers who do not have time for the full Lakes Trail (Hike 26) can find an alternative that is much shorter (2.7 miles total) but that visits many of the beautiful parklands and provides many of the expansive views that the longer trail is famous for. This is a loop trip that is partly on the Lakes Trail and partly on a cut-off called the High Lakes Trail.

The trail begins and ends at the parking area at the Reflection Lakes. For a counterclockwise trip (either way is equally good), look for the trail sign down near the lake shore and proceed to the right (east). The first part of the trail follows the Lakes Trail (Hike 26) for about 0.8 miles, measured from the highway. It skirts around the east side of Little Reflection Lake. Then it begins climbing, mostly in meadows and clumps of subalpine trees. A half mile from the start it comes to a rude log bridge that crosses little Louise Creek, often dry in late summer.

The trail angles up toward Faraway Rock (Hike 28) with nice views out to the Tatoosh peaks to the south, from the Castle on the left to Pinnacle Peak on the right. From Faraway Rock the view of Stevens Canyon is excellent. One can follow the Stevens Canyon Road's winding descent to the east and in the foreground, one looks down onto the shore of Louise Lake. The route then goes closer to another lake, Faraway Lake, which lies perched in a hollow at the edge of the canyon cliff.

A few hundred yards beyond the lake is a trail junction. The High Lakes Trail turns off to the left. It is a nearly level trail that connects the east arm of the Lakes Trail to the west arm. It is 1.2 miles in length and it stays most of its length in sub-alpine parkland, populated by flowers and berry bushes.

There is no view of Rainier, but the views of the mountains to the south, especially of Foss Peak and Unicorn, are excellent. The meadowlands are rolling and scenic. In the autumn the blueberry bushes are colorful and the berries are delicious.

The trail descends into forest near its end and then reaches a junction with the Lakes Trail. Turning left here, the route descends through mixed woods and meadow towards Reflection Lakes. En route it crosses a tiny creek on a nice bridge, with Pinnacle Peak towering above.

Soon the highway sounds announce the proximity of the trip's end at Reflection Lake. The trail includes a quarter mile of shoreline travel before it ascends to the parking lot, where crowds may be seen enjoying the mountain and its reflection.

Hikers looking for a short hike in the Reflection Lakes area might choose to go up the Lakes Trail (Hike 26) as far as Faraway Rock, only about ¾ mile one way. The beginning of this short hike is described in Hike 27.

The way to Faraway Rock is on the south side of the slope and it remains below 5200 feet, so it's often open for travel before the higher trails at Paradise are snow-free. It is not a level trail, gaining 400 feet in elevation to the Rock, but it is wide and well-maintained, suitable even for inexperienced hikers. Parents of small children should be extremely cautious at the top of the trail, as there is no fence or barrier between the trail and an 800 foot high drop-off to the lake below.

The broad graveled trail below the Rock traverses the slope to the east past huckleberry bushes and evergreens. Views of the Tatoosh range are excellent. Faraway Rock is a promontory at the end of Mazama Ridge. The view from the level rock surface to the south and east is superb.

The plentitude of trails in the Paradise-Reflection Lakes region leads to several possible loop hikes. Persons who don't like to retrace their steps can, for instance, take a loop trip from the Reflection Lakes to Narada Falls (or vice versa). Largely in forest, the trip can be a pleasant one, especially on days when wide vistas are cancelled by cloudy weather. The entire loop is about 2.6 miles long.

The following trip starts at the lakes and goes clockwise. Other options can, of course, be chosen and the description read in the appropriate order. Here we start the trip at the intersection of the Lakes Trail (Hike 26) and the Wonderland Trail (Hike 125), just west of the largest Reflection Lake.

The trail descends gradually at first, passing through a particularly beautiful open forest.

Losing altitude, the trail finds itself in increasingly dense cover. Soon it switchbacks around to the north and 1.3 miles from the lakes it comes to a trail intersection. The Wonderland Trail goes off to the left and a short spur trail goes right, to Narada Falls (Hike 11). Turn right. The trail arrives at the falls near its bottom, providing an excellent view of the main drop.

From the top of the falls, where there is a parking lot and service road, find an inconspicuous trail sign for the Narada Falls Trail to Paradise. This trail section follows the river valley gently up to the bridge that carries the Stevens Canyon Road over the Paradise River above a small waterfall.

After crossing the road, hikers will find the trail continuing on the north side of the river. In less than a quarter of a mile there is a trail junction, where the Narada Falls Trail ends. To the left is the Lakes Trail up to Paradise; to the right is the Lakes Trail back to the Reflection Lakes, which the looper should, of course, take. It's just under a mile back to the starting point.

Pinnacle Peak is a Matterhorn-shaped member of the Tatoosh Range, just south of Reflection Lakes. With a top at an elevation of 6562 feet, it isn't quite half as high as the Matterhorn, nor has it now any of the immense glaciers that surround the Matterhorn. But years ago glaciers did their thing here, carving the sides of Pinnacle Peak almost as thoroughly as glaciers carved its Swiss cousin. Mountain climbers who look up at it can't help feeling the itch to climb it and its climbing history tells of the exploits of well-known mountaineers who conquered its precipitous north face.

Normal people can also visit this peak, though "conquering it" should not be their goal,

as even its south face is a tricky ascent to be made only by experienced and well-equipped mountaineers. But there is an excellent trail, one of the Park's most popular, that leads to the high pass on the west side of Pinnacle Peak. In only 1.3 miles, hikers can reach the high meadows and the famous views at Pinnacle Saddle.

The trailhead is directly across the Steven Canyon Road from the Reflection Lakes parking lot. It is a smooth and gentle trail, suitable for small children. Mt. Rainier is behind you for most of the way up, but hikers should turn around now and then to watch it change as you go higher. The mountain seems to get higher as you move back from it and as you gain a better perspective of its immensity.

The slopes of Pinnacle Peak just above treeline provide homes for many marmots and it is common to see them lunching among the rocks or crossing a late season snow slope.

As the trail nears the peak, it breaks out into open country and steepens, becoming rocky as it crosses talus slopes. A giant switchback turns hikers so that they can see the mountain from this elevated viewpoint. Paradise Valley and its road become visible.

The trail ends at a saddle point between Pinnacle Peak and Denman Peak. Here the view to the south is inspiring. Above the deep valleys Mt. Adams and Goat Rocks are on the skyline. On a really clear day Oregon's Mt. Hood can be seen rising above the foothills to the south. To the east is the one-horned shape of Unicorn Peak.

From the saddle there is a way trail that leads farther on, down onto a rocky shelf. Not far down this path is a clear rock-bound tarn. The way trail continues on south and eventually fades away.

Turning back, it's time to head down to the road. On the way the mountain and the distant trails of Paradise fill the field of view.

Hike 31 – Plummer Peak map pg. 69

Genuinely experienced hikers who reach the Pinnacle Peak saddle might be tempted to follow a way trail, unmaintained and unofficial, to the summit of the mountain that looms above to the west, Plummer Peak. Plummer is almost as high as Pinnacle, but a little safer, as its climb doesn't involve as much steep, loose rock.

An impassioned word to hikers who leave the official trails in this National Park: the maintained trails were built to take you to hundreds of glorious destinations, but they also exist to protect the special environment of the park so that it will remain glorious for future generations to enjoy (and for the park's plant and animal life's survival). Anyone who leaves these trails should travel so that boots touch only on rock or snow, or, in the presence of a way trail, only there. This is not the place to wander off, stomping on the fragile plants of the meadows. The ugly defacing of the high country can be seen in too many places at Rainier, where networks of random paths invade the landscape. In the case of Plummer Peak, stay on the obvious way trail. It will lead to the best views by the safest route and staying on it will protect the rest of this beautiful mountain.

The path to Plummer heads right from Pinnacle saddle (Hike 30), traversing fairly steeply up the northern slopes of the peak. The high meadows of Plummer are extensive, as its summit is as flat as Pinnacle's is pointed. There are splendid views in all directions. Meadows and the sharp summit of Eagle Peak are to the west.

And this view, including Unicorn Peak, is to the east.

A mile east on the Stevens Canyon Road from Reflection Lakes is the trailhead for an exceptionally nice trail to two lovely lakes. The trail goes to Snow Lake with an intermediate stop at Bench Lake. It's only 1.25 miles to the trail end at Snow Lake, with Bench Lake a little beyond the half way point. Almost all of the trail is in open meadow country and the views along the way are superb, especially looking back at Rainier.

The trail starts abruptly up through a bit of forest and then enters the open flat area called "The Bench", hence the name of the first lake. The view ahead is of the pointed top of Unicorn Peak.

Soon the trail provides a view of Bench Lake, with the distant crest of the Cascades visible in the distance.

To reach the shore of Bench Lake it's necessary to take a short spur trail down to its level. From there one gets a nice reflected view of Rainier. After leaving Bench Lake the trail, which has been pretty level so far, goes up over a slight rocky pass, from which the views are even better. It then drops to cross a creek and heads up again towards Snow Lake.

Above the lake's west shore the trail divides, with the main trail heading on to the shoreline and a secondary trail heading to the left to Snow Lake Camp. The east side of the lake is steep, with scattered trees, but there is a flat, grassy meadow south of the lake.

Snow Lake lies at the foot of Unicorn, whose talus slopes come right down to the water's edge.

Hike 33 – Martha Falls

map pg. 68

About a mile and a half on the Stevens Canyon Road beyond the Snow Lake trailhead the road crosses the Wonderland Trail (Hike 125). There is a small sign on the right-hand side of the road and room for a car or two to park near it.

Taking the trail down to the east brings the casual hiker to one of the nicer waterfalls in the area. It is also a particularly welcome place to stop and rest for Wonderland Trail hikers ascending from the deep canyon below. About a mile down the trail, which passes through interesting shrubland before dipping down into forest, is the falls. The stream is Unicorn Creek and the source is Snow Lake and the lesser creek that rises in The Bench. The falls cascade down the face of a cliff of basaltic columns.

Box Canyon is a popular tourist stop on the Stevens Canyon Road. It is a narrow, deep cleft in the rock through which the Muddy Fork of the Cowlitz River roars. There are the usual tourist amenities (a short nature trail, restrooms, water, a picnic area) and there is a nice loop trail, about a mile and a half long, that leads down to Stevens Creek and back.

The first part of the trail is the Wonderland Trail (Hike 125) and the way back is a side trail that returns to the road near the Box Canyon Picnic Area. To do the loop, one can leave from either end. This description begins near the Box Canyon Bridge and returns to the picnic area. Either way necessitates a short tramp on the highway to complete the loop. The short nature trail starts on the north side of the road, where there are slabs of slick rock and mosses.

A few hundred yards from the highway the trail crosses the canyon on an elegant footbridge. The deep and narrow canyon is breathtaking from here, especially upstream from the bridge.

Eyond the bridge the loop trip joins the Wonderland Trail, which ascends to the left onto a ridge that carries it over the highway tunnel. It then descends along the top of this forested ridge, heading south. The Muddy Fork of the Cowlitz is in the valley to the left. After a half mile the trail turns right and drops down to Stevens Creek.

The Wonderland Trail goes on up the valley towards Martha Falls and Reflection Lakes from here, after first crossing Stevens Creek on a handsome bridge. The loop trail leaves the Wonderland just before the bridge, turning back up the slope through the quiet forest. This trail joins road at the secluded Box Canyon Picnic Area, where many of the picnic tables are hidden in the shade among the trees.

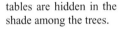

From the picnic area turn right and it's about a quarter of a mile along the road to the tunnel and the bridge. The end of the loop is at the mossy rocks that hide the river that thunders through the unique cleft of Box Canyon.

Box Canyon is the beginning of a nice forested section of the Wonderland Trail that makes a pleasant day trip. There are few distant views, so this is a trail that loses none of its charm on misty days when distant views aren't there. The trail starts just across the road from the Box Canyon parking area. Turn right at the Wonderland Trail sign.

The trip to Nickel Creek is an easy 0.8 mile through very pleasant forest. The lacy branches of Western Hemlock soften the light and the forest floor is graced by shade-loving plants, especially various kinds of ferns and groups of Vanilla Leaf. Vanilla Leaf is fairly commonly found at these altitudes, distinctive with elaborate leaves and modest white flowers.

Nickel Creek is reached quite soon after a nice forest stroll. The handsome creek is crossed on a giant log bridge.

Individual campsites are located along the creek and a group site is perched a little farther up the trail in a large clearing.

Beyond the camp the Wonderland continues on up, reaching the crest of the Cowlitz Divide in another 2.3 miles (Hike 36). Here it meets the Ollalie Creek Trail (Hike 44), turns left and heads for magnificent views from the high meadows beyond.

An especially beautiful section of the Wonderland Trail is the part that traverses the high ridge known as the Cowlitz Divide. These views are largely the privilege of the long distant hiker, as the Divide is not close to roads. One access route that makes a nice but fairly rigorous day trip is the section from Box Canyon up past Nickel Creek Camp (Hike 35) to the Divide. The first really good views are about a mile past the junction with the Ollalie Creek Trail (Hike 44), 4.5 miles from Box Canyon. The first 3.5 miles are forested and the rail becomes steep after leaving Nickel Creek, with many switchbacks.

As the trail reaches the ridge, the vegetation changes from firs and hemlocks to high altitude trees and huckleberries. Then, as it gradually ascends the ridge top, it passes through meadowland. About a mile past the Ollalie Creek Trail junction the trail reaches a more open section, providing a grand view of this side of Mt. Rainier.

The great triangular rock pointing to the summit from high in the center of the view above is Gibraltar Rock, with the Cowlitz Glacier cradled just below it. To the right is a nice view of Washington State's third highest mountain, Little Tahoma, a volcano that is a satellite peak of Rainier, rising 11,138 feet above sea level.

It's tempting to go on as the views get better and better, but it's a good distance back to the road, so it might be prudent to turn around here and head back.

The Backbone Ridge Trail is an unmaintained trail that leaves from the southernmost curve of the Stevens Canyon Road and goes basically nowhere. It's a remote and lonely part of the Park and few hikers visit it. The trail heads north, staying near the top of a ridge. There are very few views out of the forest and parts of the trail are hard to follow. The trailhead is not marked, so to find the trail it is best to follow these directions and use this photo of the trail's start as a guide.

Coming from the west, there is a sharp curve to the left about 4 miles from Box Canyon. Pull over to the large graveled area on the left and park. The trail is just this side of the crest of the ridge shown above. From the east, watch for the camera sign that indicates a view of the mountain just around the corner.

The start is through a pleasant forest, with the trail being fairly obvious at first. As it continues, however, it sometimes almost disappears in the slowly growing underbrush. Higher on the ridge there are fine examples of intermediate level open forest. A mile and a half or so from the start it comes to a rocky outcropping and turns abruptly and steeply to the right. The opening in the tree cover permits a glimpse of Mt. Rainier.

There isn't much more of the trail past the ridge top. It descends a bit and then encounters two ghost trails that are even more difficult to follow, though some maps show them descending, in one case to the left to the highway, and in the other case to the right to join an abandoned section of the Cowlitz Divide Trail. It is possible to locate the point where the latter joins the highway, but not to follow it very far.

Hike 38 – Backbone Lake

map: this page

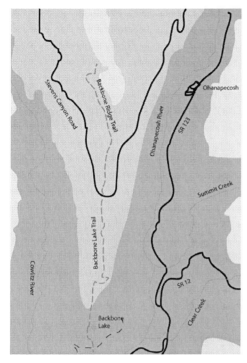

The Backbone Lake Trail is only partly within the National Park. In fact, it leaves the Park boundary after only 50 or 100 feet and the rest of it is in the Gifford Pinchot National Forest. It's an excellent trail, well-maintained, and remarkably varied, though there are few views beyond the forest until it reaches Backbone Lake.

The trailhead is directly across the Stevens Canyon Highway from that for Backbone Ridge (Hike 37). Climb up the edge of the right side of the cut made for the highway and watch for the trail. From the top of the cut is the first and last view of Mt. Rainier from this trail. The trail sign suggests that this is a continuation of the Backbone Ridge trail. It also points out that there is a Forest Service road beyond the lake and that the lake is only 0.3 miles from the road, a much shorter distance than for this trail. Such a

short trail might hint that the lake will be heavily populated by people coming in from the south. It may be on weekends. It was deserted on the sunny autumn day when these photos were taken.

This trail is upside down compared to most mountain trails. It begins at the top and goes steadily down hill to its destination. The altitude lost is about 1600 feet and the distance is 3 miles. Remember that it's all uphill after the lake.

The entire route is through virgin forest, ranging in altitude from about 3600 feet to about 2000 feet. This variation in altitude leads to a fascinating forest experience for any hiker taking the trail and taking the time to notice the changing forest understory. At the top of the route the forest is near the upper levels of the intermediate forest zone. Under the trees the growth is sparse.

However, a little lower on this trail the hiker comes to an area where the entire understory is a layer of bracken ferns, which enjoy the spots of sun at this altitude. Farther on, one comes to a section where the land under the trees is covered by a lush growth of salal. Next comes an area where the sunny places are inhabited by thick groves of vine maple.

About two miles from the trailhead the route reaches a place on the ridge top where there's a small open meadow. The view here is to the west and it's possible to see the southern Tatoosh Mountains, including Peak 6310, the location of the Tatoosh Lookout.

Finally, after taking a short side trail to the left, the hiker reaches Backbone Lake, a medium-sized forest-bound lake with camp spots on its banks, mostly at the northern end. Logs line the verge of the lake, as is typical of lowland lakes at this altitude.

Chapter 5 – The Ohanapecosh Region

Ohanapecosh is at the southeastern corner of Mt. Rainier National Park. This is the location of a park entrance via State Route 123, which connects with State Route 12, the White Pass Highway. There is a ranger station, a very nice campground and a visitor center, as well as a number of fine trails in the lush forest.

Ohanapecosh was established a hundred years ago when hot springs were discovered here and a resort was established. With the opening of the first road, coming into the area from the south, large numbers of tourists visited the resort, most seeking the fabled medical powers of the hot mineral waters. The name Ohanapecosh Hot Springs was changed in the 1920's when a physician, Dr. A. W. Bridge from Tacoma, acquired it and named it the Bridge Clinic. The resort consisted of a hotel, a bathhouse and 30 cabins.

In 1931 the boundaries of the National Park were increased to include Ohanapecosh and

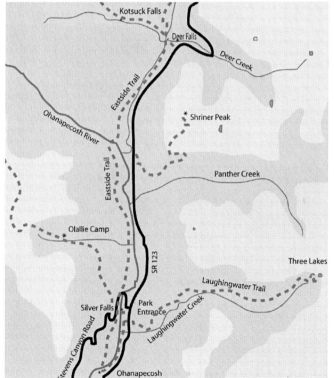

the area was gradually integrated into the Park. The resort was bought by the Park Service in the 1960s and torn down, with the hot springs being returned to their natural state. Now the area is a quiet and natural pocket of lowland forest, bisected by the beautifully clear and busy Ohanapecosh River. Several nice lowland hikes start from here.

Map 8 Ohanapecosh North

89

The Grove of the Patriarchs Trail is a short and popular nature trail that visits some of the grandest giant trees left in the Cascades. It is in the Ohanapecosh area, but its main trailhead is not actually at Ohanapecosh, though there is a trail from there to the Grove. Unless hikers are camping at Ohanapecosh, the start is more readily made from near the park entrance at Stevens Canyon. A few hundred yards inside the entrance is a parking lot on the right (or on the left for people driving down the Stevens Canyon Road from the west). This is the trailhead for both the Grove of the Patriarchs Trail and the Eastside Trail (Hike 43). There are restrooms and picnic facilities.

The Grove of the Patriarchs Trail is a loop trip 1.3 miles in total length. It shares its first few hundred yards with the Eastside Trail, before turning right to cross the Ohanapecosh River on a metal bridge.

From the bridge the view of the river is revealing of its nature. Unlike the Nisqually or the White River, the Ohanapecosh here is a clear, gentle stream.

Its valley is more gradual than the valleys of many of the others of Rainier's rivers, making it flow less tumultuously. Its waters are largely derived from snow melt, rather than glacier melt, so that the water is clear, revealing its rocky bed and reflecting the blue of the sky.

After crossing the bridge, one enters a remarkable and different world. This small section of forest is as ancient as any in the Cascades. Normally forest fires, usually started by lightning, limit the age of a forest. Every so often, once in a couple of hundred years or so, any section of forest is burned to the ground. The trees in that section are gone and the forest must start all over again from seeds brought by the wind or by birds from neighboring, undamaged woodland. This means that there are seldom any trees that are more than a couple of hundred years old in any place in the forest.

But occasionally there is a bit of forest that has escaped being devastated by fire for an unusually long time, allowing its trees to reach amazing sizes and venerable ages. The Grove of the Patriarchs is one such place. Protected by being on an island of the Ohanapecosh River, it has withstood damage by fire for at least a thousand years. The trees are among the largest of their species in the world, giant Western Red Cedars, Western Hemlocks and Douglas Firs, some as much as fifty feet in circumference.

The ground here also has seen little damage for centuries. Not until people started coming to admire the trees had it been disturbed. Over the years since the Park opened the trampling by thousands of feet began to damage the trees' surroundings, especially their roots, threatening their health for the first time in a millennium. The Park Service has responded by constructing a board walk over much of the trail, allowing us to admire the great giants without disturbing their golden years.

Rangers have counted more than 30 trees here that are more than 25 feet in circumference. Several are 300 feet tall, their tops invisible far above you as you stroll among these giants.

Around one of the largest

trees there is a wooden platform built so that visitors can get up close without trampling on the tree's roots.

The Grove of the Patriarchs is a quiet place. Visitors seem aware of its special nature as they walk silently among these magnificent ancient giants. The short hike to the Grove can be one of the highlights of any visit to the Park.

Every campground should have a short trail nearby for campers who have an extra hour to occupy or who have elected to camp with small children. Ohanapecosh has an excellent example, a nature trail, only 0.6 miles long, which visits the deep forest, the hot springs and the site of the former health settlement. The Park Service supplies a brief printed guide book at the trailhead, which describes the various highlights of the trail at 22 numbered stops. The trail starts near the Visitor Center and ends in the campground, from which it is a brief stroll back to the point of beginning. The trail is through forest and meadow.

Ohanapecosh is at an altitude of 2200 feet. At these altitudes in the Cascades, Western Hemlock is often the dominant tree, as in this forest. Hemlocks are tall, graceful trees with lacy branches of needles and with a distinctively bent top, which can be noticed even for the very young trees seen along the trail. Other evergreens in this forest include Western Red Cedar and Douglas Fir (which, actually, is not a true fir and is sometimes referred to as Douglas-Fir or douglasfir). But it is the Hemlocks that form most of the cool forest at Ohanapecosh.

Beneath the trees there is life, too. Vine maple groves, stands of hemlock saplings and occasional red huckleberry bushes fill in the middle levels and on the ground are ferns and flowering bunchberry (or Canadian dogwood).

A clearing ahead indicates that the trail has come to the hot springs.

Do not expect too much. The springs are not really very hot and they do not bubble up colorfully like those at Yellowstone. In fact it's difficult to imagine a hotel, a bathhouse and cabins here for the sake of these minor springs, but that was years ago, when people believed that there was something medicinal about sitting and soaking in these miner-laden waters. Modern medicine says that arthritis sufferers might just as well stay home and soak in their bathtubs, so PLEASE stay on the trail.

The hot water is actually cooler than a summer day in Phoenix, but it is warm enough to dissolve some of the minerals out of the rocks that it passes through below ground, where it is being heated up. These minerals are probably the main reason that there is a meadow here. The native plants don't like to grow in caustic (to them) environments.

A nearby deep depression in the ground is about the only evidence left of the existence of a resort here. It was dug out with the intention of putting in a swimming pool, but the project was never completed.

At a trail junction ahead take the trail to the left to return to Ohanapecosh. The right-hand trail goes upslope 2 miles to Silver Falls (Hike 41). After passing another small meadow, the nature trail continues to the attractive Ohanapecosh campground. Turn left and follow the road back to the Visitor Center.

One of the great rewards of a visit to Ohanapecosh is the trail trip to Silver Falls. It's a loop trip, nearly level, and only about 2.7 miles total in length. Its highlight is magnificent Silver Falls, where the Ohanapecosh River drops 40 feet over mossy rocks into a deep pool beneath the trail. One usually starts the trip on the east side of the river, where the trailhead is shared with the nature trail near the Visitor Center. The loop goes upriver to the falls, crosses the river and returns down along the west side, to arrive at the campground across a bridge from the start. There are no distant views on this trip, which makes it a nice choice to make on a cloudy day.

Mt. Rainier National Park is well endowed with waterfalls. The abundant rainfall and snowfall, combined with the steep slopes at both high and intermediate elevations, means that rivers and streams frequently find themselves forced to jump over cliffs, down to the

next level. There are more than 70 waterfalls identified on Park USGS maps. Only a few have names (mostly the largest ones and those near roads or trails). The highest is Comet Falls (Hike 12) and the one with the longest name is Wauhaukaupauken Falls, near Indian Bar (Hike 61).

The trail begins by following the nature trail (Hike 40) through the deep forest.

At 0.2 miles there is a junction. The nature trail goes left and the falls trail goes right, crossing a couple of streams that come down from the east to flow into the Ohanapecosh. The largest of these streams is Laughingwater Creek, aptly named because of its spirited and noisy descent through the forest. It is a mile from the trailhead.

It's only 0.2 miles farther, up and over a ridge, to where the first sight and sound of Silver Falls is reached.

The trail traverses along a steep cliff with a guard rail to prevent hikers from falling to their death by slipping on the rocks kept slippery by the falls' spray.

The trail swings around to the left and crosses the river on a high bridge, affording a good view of the river's narrow, rocky canyon downstream.

Going north a bit, the trail comes to a close-up of the falls above it. Then it arrives at the first of two nearby trail junctions. This one is for the Eastside Trail (Hike 43), which continues north all the way to Cayuse Pass, with intermediate stops at the Stevens Canyon Road, the Grove of the Patriarchs (Hike 39) and the Deer Creek area (Hike 46).

Keep left to stay on the Silver Falls loop. Only a few hundred yards farther is another junction, this one with a trail that heads north, crosses the Stevens Canyon Road and continues up to the Ollalie Creek Camp and on to the Cowlitz Divide (Hike 36). Keep left again and follow the trail along the west side of the river back to Ohanapecosh.

The trail stays above the river, seldom within sight of it. At one point it passes beneath a rocky outcropping before descending back to the campground.

At the campground turn left again and walk over the bridge to the Visitor Center, completing the loop.

The Laughingwater Trail is hidden away in the southeast corner of the Park where few visitors come. It is a quiet trail that rambles through nice forest and occasional meadows, ultimately reaching three peaceful lakes, nestled in the woods near timberline. The distance to the lakes is about 6 miles.

The trail goes on to meet the Pacific Crest Trail outside the Park boundary. It's about 2 miles beyond the lakes to the boundary and there are many nice destinations nearby in the National Forest. Hikers who camp at Three Lakes might consider making it a complete set by hiking a couple of miles along the crest trail to Two Lakes and then taking off cross country to the east to One Lake.

The Laughingwater trailhead is at the Ohanapecosh Visitor Center. From there one takes the Silver Falls Trail (Hike 41) a little over a mile to Laughingwater Creek, where the trail takes off to the right. A shortcut can be used if there's a place to park on the Eastside Highway 1 ½ miles north of the Ohanapecosh turn-off, where the trail crosses the road. There's a trail sign there at the edge of the road.

The first part of the trail climbs up through a nice forest of Western Hemlock and Douglas Fir. A mile and a half from the highway it comes to some nice wetlands. Watch for wildlife (at least some deer) in this more open section.

Soon it's back in the woods, which are gradually changing character as elevation is gained. There are more hemlocks and the beginnings of subalpine species appear.

At about 4800 feet the trail climbs over a low pass and gently drops to the banks of the first of the Three Lakes.

It swings around the south side of this quiet lake and comes upon a rustic patrol cabin, situated under the trees near Lake No. 2.

Three Lakes Camp is located near the patrol cabin and the third lake is located a little farther on, towards the trail that exits the Park.

The lake shores are inviting places to rest and contemplate the happy fact that this area was added to the park and to wonder how such a peaceful place can remain so in this increasingly crowded world.

The Eastside Trail is one of the best forest trails in the Northwest – We'd even nominate it for one of the best in the world. What makes it so special? First, it visits a pristine, virgin forest of a type that has all but disappeared. There are only a few islands of Pacific Northwest forest that have been spared from logging. Mt. Rainier National Park is one of the best of these islands and the Eastside Trail passes through one of its nicest examples. Second, it is a long enough trail that a visitor can become fully immersed in the forest environment. There are other fine forest trails in the Park, but none as long as this one.

Third, it is a gentle, beautifully maintained trail, nearly level over most of its length, so that users can concentrate on the nature around them, not on the struggle up some steep hillside. And last, it is a lonely trail, hiked only by the few who know and treasure its unique quality. The summer crowds of other parts of the Park are unknown here. Of course, we hope that if you discover this trail you'll keep quiet about it!

There are several places that can be called the trailhead for this trail. This description starts at the parking area near the Stevens Canyon Entrance, near the Grove of the Patriarchs (Hike 39). It follows the trail to the Deer Creek Camp, a distance of 7 miles of uninterrupted forest trekking. Another section continues north from Deer Creek to Cayuse Pass (Hike 49) and a last section continues on up to Chinook Pass (Hike 48). It is also possible to add more miles by starting lower down, at Ohanapecosh, taking the Silver Falls Trail (Hike 41) and a spur trail on to the highway. If all of these options are included, the total length of the trip is 16 miles one way.

This is a trail of waterfalls. Creeks and rivers come tumbling down from the left, most with their origins in snowfields and glaciers high on the slopes of the mountain. Most falls are not officially named, but the first one, a little over a mile from the trailhead, is a falls of Olallie Creek, so it is referred to unofficially as Olallie Falls.

Giant trees and lush undergrowth mark off each step, but creeks and bridges mark off the miles. Some creeks earn only a carefully-placed log bridge for the crossing. Other streams are no bigger, but have nice wide bridges.

Bridges and creeks are rare, however, compared to the multitude of giant trees. A little more than 3 miles from the trailhead is a spectacular example, a Douglas fir that looks

big enough to hollow out for a three bedroom home (perhaps a small one with three stories). It's just above the trail at its only switchback, where it climbs a little in order to cross the Ohanapecosh River.

Until this point, the trail has followed the valley of the Ohanapecosh, though seldom close enough to see the river. Here it crosses the river, which turns left and heads up to Ohanapecosh Park and the glaciers above. As you near the river, its noise seems unusually intense. There's a bridge ahead. But this is no ordinary bridge. The trail builders crossed the river in a breathtaking way, on a bridge that spans the river where it plunges over a marvelous 75 foot waterfall.

Beyond the Ohanapecosh Falls Bridge the trail continues north, now following the valley of Chinook Creek, whose headwaters are far above at Chinook Pass. The forest remains quiet and friendly.

At least it's quiet for a while. A mile and a half from the Ohanapecosh Falls Bridge the noise level increases, suggesting that another waterfall is nearby. Watch for a short spur trail to the right; it leads down to a viewpoint for 40 foot-high Stafford Falls.

A half mile beyond Stafford Falls the trail crosses to the other side of Chinook Creek. Its clear water indicates that it does not come from a glacier, but from snowmelt and springs.

Seven miles from the start the Eastside Trial reaches a crossroads. The trail to the left goes uphill to Kotsuck Falls (Hike 47), Owyhigh Lakes (Hike 58) and the White River entrance road. The trail to the right goes up steeply past Deer Creek Falls (Hike 46) to the Eastside Highway. And the trail straight ahead, a continuation of the Eastside Trail, goes up to Cayuse Pass. Deep in the woods near the intersection is Deer Creek Camp, not far from the trail.

This area is well worth exploring, as the confluence of the trails makes it easy to enjoy the confluence of three creeks and several unnamed but interesting waterfalls.

The hike to Ollalie Creek Camp can be a lonely one. The trail is not widely used, though it passes through miles of attractive forest. This may be because there are no wide views between the start and the camp's position, which is 3.8 miles from the trailhead. People who want wide views, however, can go on to the junction with the Wonderland Trail, another mile and a quarter, and proceed up along the Cowlitz Divide to tremendous viewpoints (Hikes 36 and 125).

The trailhead is on the Stevens Canyon Road about a mile up from the Stevens Canyon Entrance. There's a small parking area and a trail sign (which is labeled Cowlitz Divide Trail). Campers at Ohanapecosh can use an alternate trailhead at the campground, following either route to Silver Falls (Hike 41) and then a short connecting trail to the Ollalie Creek Trail.

The trail is mostly in woods. It climbs gradually along the side of a ridge to the left until it comes to the Ollalie Creek Valley, when it bears left and goes west up the valley.

Forest lovers will like this trail. It is soft under foot, cool on hot days and not very steep. Interesting things can be found by alert eyes that scan the forest floor.

A small unnamed creek, which flows down from a small unnamed lake, is crossed on an old log bridge.

Eventually the trail nears Olallie Creek and it comes to a fairly inconspicuous trail sign, indicating the side trail to Olallie Creek Camp.

The camp is in fairly open forest next to the creek. Cross a log to reach it.

The east side of the Park has many splendid trails, but for views the Shriner Peak Trail is hard to beat. On a clear day the trail provides panoramas of Rainier and the surrounding Cascades that are so marvelous that the trail length (4.2 miles) and the elevation gain (3400 feet) seem well worth it. Because it is largely in the open past the first mile and a half, it can be hot on a warm summer day. In the autumn it is cooler and the views are just as good.

The trailhead is off the Eastside Highway (State Route 123), 3½ miles north of the

Stevens Canyon Entrance Station. The trail is on the east side of the road; parking along the highway is on the left a little ways from the trail. The first half mile of trail passes through a characteristic deep forest, with only occasional sunny breaks in the green cover. This side of Shriner Peak experienced a forest fire many years ago and the forest soon opens up to reveal the edge of the burned area, marked by blackened tree stumps.

Next comes a new forest, in which regeneration has begun. Pioneer inhabitants include young evergreens, but deciduous trees and shrubs predominate, including Vine Maple. This part of the trail is especially nice in the fall when it's cool and leaves are yellow and gold.

Openings in the trees provide great views of the Ohanapecosh valley and distant mountains to the south. Directly south is the valley of Panther Creek, which flows from the Cascade Crest west to join the Ohanapecosh River. Rising above it in the view from the trail is Sheep Mountain, 5131 feel high, and near its top is little Sheep Lake, which can be reached on an abandoned trail from near the Three Lakes (Hike 42). The top of Sheep Mountain is rounded and forested.

Higher on the trail the trees are smaller and the views are more open. The vegetation is mostly bracken ferns, blueberries and a sprinkling of Subalpine Firs. Looking south, the valley opens up to peaks beyond, which belong to the western end of the Goat Rocks area.

Soon the view to the west opens up, too, and there is the first view of Rainier. The view of the mountain from this side is considered by many to be the best because of its symmetry. Little Tahoma, which spoils the symmetry from the south and north, is in the foreground and the slopes down from each side of Rainier's summit are nearly symmetrical.

As the trail gets higher another symmetrical mountain becomes visible in the south, Mt. Adams, whose rounded, snowy peak is 40 miles away.

To the right of Rainier is a good view of the Cowlitz Chimneys. These pinnacles are popular climbing destinations, reached from the White River/Sunrise Road via the Owyhigh Lakes Trail (Hike 58). The highest peak is 7605 feet in elevation.

The trail remains in open country to the summit. It winds around a shoulder of the mountain at about 5000 feet, where there is a broad valley that is often occupied by elk. At least their tracks will be here.

Shriner Peak is one of the circle of fire lookouts that formerly, before aerial and satellite surveillance, were the lifeline of fire prevention in the Park. Unlike the case of Forest Service lookouts, most of which have been torn down, the Park Service maintains its lookouts, partly because of their historic and scenic significance and partly because they make good summer residences for Park personnel, usually volunteers, who meet and serve visiting hikers.

The lookout's wrap-around deck is a perfect place for taking in the expansive views in all directions. There is Mt. Rainier, of course, to the west.

To the northwest are the Cowlitz Chimneys and prickly Governor's Ridge. The distant peaks of Chinook Pass mark the northern horizon. The eastern horizon shows the bumpy crest of the Cascade Range. South is the trail to the Shriner Peak Camp and beyond it, Mt. Adams and Goat Rocks. In the southwest some of the peaks of the Tatoosh Range are visible. And the view down from this high perch is of the flanks of Shriner Peak and the valley, to which hikers must return, probably reluctantly, to their cars.

Hike 46 - Deer Creek Falls

map pg. 89

The trail to Deer Creek Falls provides a nice short hike to a nice tall waterfall. The falls are about 80 feet tall, depending on where one measures them, and are only a few hundred feet from the trailhead. To start the trip, watch for the trail sign about 6 miles north of the Stevens Canyon Entrance (or a little over 4 miles from Cayuse Pass). It's on the west side of the road and parking is down hill a bit and on the east side.

The trail is called the Owyhigh Lakes Trail because it continues past the falls, down to

the bottom of the valley and then up again to a high pass near Barrier Peak. From there it descends to the two Owyhigh Lakes (Hike 58) and on downhill again to the road near the White River Entrance. At the bottom of the valley, just 0.4 miles from the trailhead, the trail intersects two other trails. To the left is the Eastside Trail (Hike 43), which heads down river, south to Ohanapecosh. To the right is the Upper Eastside Trail (Hike 49), which goes up to Highway 123 near Cayuse Pass. There's a little-known continuation trail that goes farther up, eventually reaching Chinook Pass (Hike 48).

The trail begins descending immediately, following Deer Creek down to where it meets

Chinook Creek. The forest seems unusually dark.

As one goes down through the dense forest, the sound of the creek on the right gradually increases in volume. The reason, of course, is that the falls is getting closer. Switchbacks bring hikers nearer and then farther from the creek, until a final switchback brings them right up to a splendid view of Deer Creek Falls.

The falls are best, of course, in the early summer, when the snow above is rapidly melting. The left-hand photograph below was taken in late June when the water was roaring down the many steps of the falls. By September the falls are quieter, but still enjoyable, as shown in the right-hand photograph.

Hike 47 - Kotsuck Falls map pg. 89

One of the biggest, noisiest and most spectacular waterfalls in the Park is thundering Kotsuck Falls. However, it suffers from two misfortunes. First, its name is awkward. How is it pronounced? And even if you know how, do you really want to? It looks like it must be an Indian name, but even Edmund Meany's list of place names (in his book, MOUNT RAINIER: A RECORD OF EXPLORATION, published in 1916) claimed its origin to be unknown.

Its second problem is that it's difficult to get a good look at it. If one knows just where to look, it is possible to make it out in the distance from the Eastside Highway, but it's merely a white smudge marking the center of the distant valley.

The trail to take is either the Owyhigh Lakes Trail (Hike 58) from the north or the section of that trail to Deer Creek Falls (Hike 46) from the south. The latter is the shorter route, bringing you to the falls from the road in only about 1½ miles. From the trail intersection at the bottom of Deer Creek, take the trail across the bridge and then go straight ahead along Kotsuck Creek to the falls. Several creeks are crossed en route.

After about a mile from the trail intersection it is clear that there's something special nearby. The trail brings one close enough that the waterfall's immense noise is heard and the vibrations it causes of the ground are felt, but it isn't seen from the trail. One has to leave the trail, cross a small valley and climb to a perilous overlook to appreciate it up close. It is not recommended to get too close to the edge; the unstable shaking of the cliff suggests that it could fall to the boiling waters below with only a slight nudge. If you do leave the trail, USE CAUTION.

The Chinook Pass Region

Chinook Pass is just barely in the Park, but it is nevertheless a heavily-visited tourist center and a trailhead for many fine hiking trips. Its popularity is partly owing to the beautiful meadows and lakes that are frequently pictured in Mt. Rainier literature and partly to the fact that it is on a major highway, SR 410, the Mather Memorial Parkway, which connects the western half of the state with the half that's east of the mountains.

At the Pass there's a small picnic area and several short trails that allow people who have only an hour or so available to take advantage of the glorious parkland and views. In mid-summer the flowers are out, wildlife is commonly encountered and the National Park experience is in full bloom.

The boundary between Rainier National Park and Snoqualmie National Forest lies exactly at the top of the pass, where the highway goes under a huge log trail bridge. On the east side, the mountains appear dry and the trees sparse, while on the west the forests are deep and wet. This section of the book includes some trails that leave the Park temporarily and others that lie entirely just outside its boundary. All are in the high country with splendid views.

There is a cluster of mountain peaks at Chinook Pass, all extending above tree line to elevations of about 6500 feet. The closest to the Pass are Yakima Peak on the north, which looms above the picnic area, and Naches Peak on the south, which is the centerpiece of an excellent loop trial (Hike 51). It is shown from the north in this photograph.

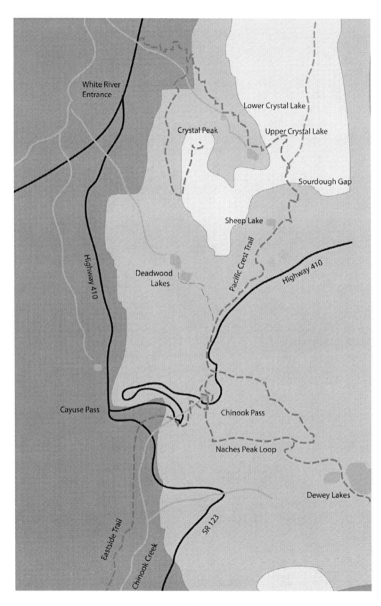

Map 9 Chinook Pass

Hike 48 – The Cayuse to Chinook Trail map pg. 118

A pleasant short trail that hardly anyone knows about is the continuation of the Eastside Trail above its intersection with Highway 123 near Cayuse Pass. It's a really nice way to arrive at Chinook Pass, as you come upon the high meadows on foot after a modest ascent from below. The trail is a little less than 1½ miles long, so it makes an excellent afternoon's round trip, especially rewarding if taken, as it is described below, from Cayuse up to Chinook and back.

Finding the lower trailhead can be a bit of a challenge, as its sign is small and inconspicuous. One drives south from the Cayuse Pass intersection of Highways 123 and 410 about 0.6 miles. There is a broad graveled parking area on the right. Across the highway from this and a hundred or so feet farther south the trail begins. It starts up a low ridge just to the left of a small valley.

The beginning of the trail is through a nice mid-elevation forest with many sunbreaks. Nice examples of forest bridges carry the trail across creeks, some of them pretty dry by summer's end.

An opening in the forest provides a view to the north of Highway 410. This road was built in the days of ambitious mountain road building, when considerations of the effects on the environment, especially the visual environment, were secondary. An immense cut in the mountainside was made in order to bring the road to the high pass. Its scar is visible from all over the east side of the Park.

About half way up the trail it encounters the road at a very pretty meadow, lush with huckleberry and blueberry bushes and seasonal flowers.

Above this meadow the trail once again leaves the road and passes through an increasingly alpine-like forest. Finally near the top the trail levels out and breaks into the open Chinook Pass meadows.

Across the road from the Cayuse-Chinook Trail (Hike 48) is an equally obscure and lonely trail, the extension of the Eastside Trail from Deer Creek Camp up to Highway 123. The trailhead is found with some difficulty, located just below the road on the west, with its sign nestled below the roadway. It's just a few hundred yards south of the large parking area described in Hike 48.

It's 3.7 miles down to the intersection with the Owyhigh Lakes Trail at Deer Creek, where a trail to the left goes up to meet the road again (Hike 46). The lakes are off to the right (Hike 58). The rest of the Eastside Trail goes on south to its end.

The trail is entirely in sunsplashed forest (in good weather; in bad weather a different kind of splash is likely) and is comfortable and quiet. If taken from the top trailhead, the elevation loss is 1400 feet, a moderate slope. A cool day's hike would be a trip down and back though there isn't much to see other than majestic trees. There is also plenty of beautiful leafy undergrowth and sometimes deer and a few Douglas squirrels.

There are also some waterfalls. A particularly large one in Chinook Creek is seen (in the distance) about a half mile from the trail end, when the trail has its only switchback. More easily seen are the several smaller waterfalls that occur at the bottom of this trail, where it encounters Deer Creek and Kotsuck Creek and there are bridges and waterfalls, seemingly in every direction.

Chinook Pass' most popular short hike is a loop trip that goes around the larger of the two Tipsoo Lakes. It is nearly impossible to drive to Chinook Pass without getting out of the car and taking this ½ mile hike. It takes the hiker to famous views of the mountain, its symmetric, glacier-covered face reflected in the sometimes still waters.

The lake basin is often crowded with tourists, but otherwise pleasant at any time of the year. In late spring (May or June) it is likely to be under several feet of snow. The highway is usually closed throughout the winter.

A favorite place to start the trail is the picnic area, just west of the lakes. After finishing off the fried chicken and watermelon, one can start the trip by hiking past the Mather Memorial, picturing the first director of the National Park Service, Stephen Mather.

From here the trail goes east past the smaller Tipsoo Lake.

One can then choose to go ether right or left around the larger lake. If right, the trail goes south towards the highway.

In summer (July and August) the lakes are surrounded by fields of flowers. In fall (September and October) the meadows are golden, the color of the dried meadow grass and seed pods of the flowers.

By far the best trail trip in the Chinook Pass region is the one that encircles Naches Peak. The trip is almost all above timberline and on a fine day it provides spectacular views of the Cascade Range in all directions. The way is nearly level all the way and the path is wide and smooth. The trail is almost exactly half in the National Park and half in the National Forest, an excellent example of effective interagency synergy. The top of the pass and the border between Park and Forest is marked by a large footbridge that spans the highway.

The loop is five miles long, making it a comfortable day trip or even a nice afternoon stroll. It can be taken in either direction, of course, but the clockwise route (as seen from above) is probably the better choice, as it provides a longer period of views of Mt. Rainier.

The trailhead can be found either at Tipsoo Lake or at the top of the highway at Chinook Pass. Just east of the pass is a large parking area with restrooms and trailheads for this and other trails, including Hikes 52, 53, 54, and 55. These destinations are reached from the Cascade Crest Trail, which is the northern part of the Pacific Crest Trail, the famous mountain trail that reaches from the Mexican to the Canadian border. While on this part of the Naches Peak loop trip it is not unusual to meet long distance hikers, who by the time they reach here in the fall, appear remarkably fit and tan.

Park in the paved lot and go up the access trail to the Crest Trail and turn left. Naches Peak, 6452 high, rises above the trail to the south. The trail beneath the north and east slopes of the peak will be visible ahead. The mountain on the right, above the trail, is

Yakima Peak, 6226 feet high. In a quarter mile or so the trail reaches the Chinook Pass footbridge. Look back for a last glimpse of Rainier before Naches Peak's mass intervenes. Yakima Peak is to its right.

The trail proceeds along the flank of Naches Peak towards the south, mostly in high meadows and clumps of trees. In summer it is bordered by flowers, especially red Indian paintbrush and white squaw grass. In fall the autumn colors are spectacular and the trail on the north side of the peak may well have snow here and there.

An open shoulder on the east side of Naches Peak is graced by a mountain tarn that reflects the peaks beyond. Although there are unofficial way trails down to the lake, please stay on the well-established path, as the meadow here is fragile and easily suffers long-term damage from only a few misplaced boots.

To the south from here the view is dominated by 6337 foot high Seymour Peak, named for a mayor of Tacoma who climbed Rainier in 1892. Dewey Lake (Hike 52) is visible beneath it.

As the trail comes around the circle to the south, the southern Cascades dominate the horizon. The mountains of the Goat Rocks Wilderness Area stand out above the sea of lesser peaks.

There is a trail junction on the south side of Naches Peak. The Cascade Crest trail turns left to descend to Dewey Lakes on its way south to Mexico and the loop trail continues to the right on its way back to Chinook Pass. A nice place for a lunch stop is the warm shelf where a small lake is set among the meadows and groves of Subalpine Firs.

Only a little farther on is the first full view of Mt. Rainier, rising above the valley of Chinook Creek and the sharp tips of the Cowlitz Chimneys and Governor's Ridge.

The trail turns again to the right, giving a little different view of Rainier. The open slopes fall away to the left towards the deep forest. In the fall these meadows are sometimes full of robins, which come up from the lowlands to feast on the sweet, ripe blueberries. As the

trail nears the highway at Chinook Pass it circles around a hidden lake, only a few hundred yards from the Tipsoo Lakes, but only visible to trail users. It is nested in a hollow beneath the western slopes of Naches Peak.

Beyond the lake the trail drops abruptly to Highway 410 and loop hikers will cross the

road and descend to the Tipsoo Lakes Trail (Hike 50). To return to the parking lot at the top of Chinook Pass, one must follow the lake loop to the far side of the larger lake, where there is a trail junction. Take the trail that heads up the open slope to the north. It swings around to the east, providing excellent views of the lake and highway below.

The trail up enters a wooded area and emerges at the top at the Cascade Crest Trail. A left turn will lead back to the Forest Service parking area.

The Dewey Lakes are a popular Chinook Pass destination, reached in about one mile from the western part of the Naches Peak Loop Trail (Hike 51). They lie just outside the National Park boundary and are therefore cared for by the good people of the Wenatchee National Forest (for some reason this is true even though they exist within the limits of the Mt. Baker Snoqualmie National Forest).

To hike to the lakes from Chinook Pass, one must take the Naches Peak Loop Trail, going either way, to a trail junction about 1 ½ miles from the Pass. An alternate route comes up from Highway 410 at a point about 7 miles east of the Pass, where a 6 mile trail follows the American River up to the lakes.

If approaching via the Loop Trail, one encounters a trail junction, with the Dewey Lakes Trail turning to the south and heading down. This is the Pacific Crest Trail. The trip to the lakes is all downhill from here. Initially there are views to the south.

Soon the trail switchbacks to the east and drops into woods. Before long it levels out as it reaches the lake basin. The Dewey Lakes are two fairly large lakes with two little tarns lying between them. These tarns are the hiker's first clue that the lakes are near.

The smaller Dewey Lake is off to the right, barely visible from the trail. The larger Dewey Lake is reached soon after on the left of the main trail. A loop trail circumnavigates the larger lake, but the PCT stays along its western shore.

Inviting beaches line the southern edge of the lake, where there are some excellent spots for lunch.

A trail junction is near the southern corner of the lake. The Crest Trail continues on past a shallow pond under massive Seymour Peak.

The outlet for the lake is around to the east on the alternate trail. A log jam often clogs the outlet, making a picturesque foreground for the view of Mt. Rainier, which just barely pokes its head above the forest ridge.

What are the Deadwood Lakes doing in this trail book? They're not on a maintained trail, they're not in the guidebooks and hardly anyone's ever heard of them. Well, that's why they're here. These two charming lakes are at the head of a small quiet valley, hidden from the crowds of Chinook Pass by an intervening ridge. They are not well known in spite of being only a mile and a half from a busy trail thoroughfare. Finding them is tricky but it's worth the effort, as there is likely to be solitude along the way and on their sandy shores.

The unmarked trail to the Deadwood Lakes leaves the Pacific Crest Trail about a half mile north of Chinook Pass. One must watch for a faint trail that heads up a small ridge to the left of the main trail. The way is up along a small valley through open slopes, rich with flowers in summer and blessed with grand views south to the Pass and Naches Peak. Near the top of the ridge there's a view of distant Mt. Adams.

Only partial views of Mt. Rainier are seen, as the bulk of Yakima Peak and its northern ridge are in the way. Looking north from the pass one sees the Sourdough Mountains with Sunrise Ridge in front of them and the bright scar of a switchback on the Sunrise Highway.

The two lakes soon are laid out below as on a map and the trail goes down quickly to meet them.

The south lake comes first. It is slightly higher than its sibling lake; both are near 5200 feet in elevation. The south lake's approach is through a lush, wet meadow.

Although it's generally fairly deep, near the shore the lake has a shallow shelf and the pure, clear water reveals an accumulation of water-logged branches of trees and bushes.

A short trail takes the hiker through the trees to the northern lake. Camping is not allowed and visitors should tread lightly, if at all, on the parklands and shores. Meadows and woods and sandy beaches are here at these two lonely lakes. They are to be found with a certain amount of difficulty and to be enjoyed with a large amount of care and discretion.

Hike 54 – Sheep Lake

map pg. 118

Although not within the National Park, Sheep Lake is popular with Park visitors, as it is a very pretty lake, reached on a nearly level, scenic trail from Chinook Pass. As the crow flies, it is only 1/3 mile from the Park boundary. Unless you're a crow, however, you will want to take the trail, which reaches the lake in a pleasant 1.9 miles from the Chinook Pass parking lot. The route is on the Pacific Crest Trail, which heads northward from the Pass by traversing the open slope of the American River Valley just above Highway 410.

The best place to begin this hike is the large, paved National Forest parking lot just east of the Chinook Pass summit. Hike up a path from the lot to the Crest Trail, which is marked by a very small sign. The trail, however, is large. It starts out as a broad, well-maintained hikers' boulevard. Turn right and begin the trip.

The first mile of this hike is almost level and remains in the open with constant views to the lovely valley below and peaks in all directions. After a mile the route turns left and begins to climb up into the open woods towards the ridge to the north. Near the lake the trail levels and flat meadows greet the hiker.

A tramp through these pleasant park-like meadows and woods soon brings one to the lake, which is set on a broad level shelf. The lake is heavily used by both campers and day hikers, so solitude is unlikely.

Perhaps the lake will be shared with others, including young children, dogs (it is not in the National Park) and maybe horses, but this should not detract much from enjoying the beauty of this shimmering jewel of an alpine lake.

Hikers to Sheep Lake (Hike 54) can look up from the lake to a notch in the wall of cliffs to the north and probably find it hard to resist the trail trip to that notch, which is named Sourdough Gap. It's only about 1¼ miles farther on the Crest Trail and the views from there are especially grand. The total distance from Chinook Pass is 3.2 miles.

Above the lake the trail meanders among stately Subalpine Firs, which seem scattered at random on the open slopes. Rising above the trail to the north is an unnamed mountain that is unofficially called Peak 6708, based on its mapped elevation.

Sourdough Gap is a fairly narrow pass, trampled by feet to a level sandy platform. The view out to the north from the Gap includes the Pacific Crest Trail, which makes its way along the nearly treeless slopes to Bear Gap, 3 miles away. To the east is the Morse Creek Valley and almost hidden Placer Lake. The view to the south is expansive. From right to left are Chinook Pass, Naches Peak, Mt. Adams, Goat Rocks and Seymour Peak. Sheep Lake lies below.

There's another trail here, one that doesn't show up on most maps. It leaves the Crest Trail near the Gap and ascends to the left to a notch among the peaks.

The trail enters the National Park at the notch and then heads down the farther slope to the Crystal Lakes (Hike 57). Taking the trail down a little way is rewarding, as there is a knoll off to the left that provides an excellent place to have lunch with a view of Upper Crystal Lake and Rainier.

Not strictly at Chinook Pass, this hike is found on Highway 410 between the Park's northern boundary and the Pass. The trailhead is 4 ½ miles inside the boundary and about ½ mile south of the turn-off for the White River Entrance Station. Parking is limited; there's a small lot on the left, next to the trailhead, and more parking across the road.

There are several uses of the word "crystal" in the region. There are the beautiful Crystal Lakes (Hike 57), reached from the same trailhead. They are the source for Crystal Creek. There is Crystal Peak, the goal of this trail description. And there is Crystal Mountain to the north, site of an extensive ski resort. Crystal Peak and Crystal Mountain are two different geographical features located about two miles from each other. There are trails to the top of each, but access to Crystal Mountain is from the ski area road, which turns off of Highway 410 just before the Park Boundary. Crystal Peak is in the National Park and it provides more of a wilderness experience (there are no ski lift towers or ski "trails" on it). Of course, the most common crystals found at either peak or on the lakes are the abundant winter-time crystals of frozen water.

The trail begins along Crystal Creek and stays in forest for most of the first 2 miles of this 4 mile trail. Elevation is gained fairly quickly by means of 10 switchbacks up the forested slopes, following the valley of Crystal Creek, which remains pretty much out of reach to the south of the trail. Occasional glimpses of the White River valley to the north are provided by avalanche clearings. Views to the west are of the upper White River and the mountain whose Emmons Glacier gives rise to its turbulent waters.

At about 1½ miles from the highway there is a trail junction. Turn right. The trail to the Peak soon crosses Crystal Creek and continues among trees, which gradually give way to the open, sunny slopes of the mountain. This is a particularly nice trail trip in late summer or autumn, when the sun is cooler and the mountain blueberries are ripe.

With the opening of the forest there are views of surrounding mountains, such as the Cowlitz Chimneys in the west. To the south are the peaks of the Chinook Pass area. To the west, above the White River, is the "backwards c-shaped" bare spot where the Sunrise highway makes a switchback turn. Above that are the peaks of the Sourdough Mountain range.

After ascending gradually along the peak's open slopes towards the south, the trail makes a sharp turn to the north, providing hikers a new set of distant views. The upper slopes are inhabited by a "ghost forest", made up of the silvery trunks of dead trees that were killed by a long-ago forest fire.

The official trail ends just short of the summit at the site of a former lookout cabin. The peak is a short scramble from there. Commanding the view from the top, of course, is Mt. Rainier.

In the opposite direction there are also nice things to see. To the east is Upper Crystal Lake, set in its high basin under rugged peaks.

Directly below the peak, just past the toes of your boots, is Lower Crystal Lake with the ridge of Crystal Mountain above it. The view south is of the valley of Chinook Creek and the Ohanapecosh River, with the Tatoosh Mountains on the horizon. The view north is of the broad White River Valley.

Lovers of Mt. Rainier National Park tend to have their favorite lake in the Park. There are many beautiful lakes and all are individuals. Big or little, high or low, forested or meadow-set, the lakes are special places. And one of the most special is Upper Crystal Lake, which is the favorite of many hikers.

Upper and Lower Crystal Lakes are less than a mile apart and yet they are quite different in character. Upper Lake shimmers in the sun in a broad open basin, surrounded by fields of flowers, berry bushes and a few alpine trees and towered over by rugged peaks. Lower Lake, on the other hand, lies in a quiet forest setting with trees right down to the shore and logs in the shallows.

The total trail distance to Upper Crystal Lake is 3.3 miles. The trailhead for the lakes is described in the Hike 56 section, as the first part of the trail, the deep forest part, is shared with the Crystal Peak Trail.

After 1.3 miles the trails diverge, the lakes trail turning to the left up the slope. The forest thins as altitude is gained. The ubiquitous wild huckleberry bushes begin to dominate the undergrowth. A few forest openings allow views out to the northwest.

Just short of 3 miles from the trailhead, there is a spur trail to the right leading in a few hundred yards to Lower Crystal Lake. Crystal Peak looms above the lake.

In the woods to the west of the lake is a small camp area. The lake and camp tend to be quiet areas, as most hikers head for the upper lake.

The trail from lower to upper lake is all in open meadow, with flowers everywhere in summer and with flaming fall colors later in the season. The trail is sandy and exceptionally comfortable.

Upper Crystal Lake is a truly park-like lake, located at an elevation of 5828 feet and surrounded by parkland and clumps of sub-alpine firs. There is a small hikers' camp nearby.

Chapter 7 - The White River Region

The White River begins its life under the great Emmons Glacier, Mt. Rainier's largest sheet of ice. Flowing out from its tunnel at the bottom of the glacier, the river is heavily laden with fine white powder called rock flour, the product of the glacier's grinding. The rock flour gives the river its distinctive white color and its name.

The White River basin within the National Park includes an entrance station, the lower part of the Sunrise Highway, the White River Campground and several trailheads. The road's altitude is modest, ranging from 3400 feet at the White River Ranger Station to 4200 feet at the campground. The entrance is usually open fairly early in the summer, but the upper part of the Sunrise Highway often is not clear of snow until June or July.

Trails in the region go up from the road, all of them to the south towards the mountain. The first, the Owyhigh Lakes Trail (Hike 58), leaves the road just 2 miles past the entrance station and the last, the White River-Burroughs Mountain Loop (Hike 65), originates at the White River Campground. All begin in the forest and rise into the open meadows of the northern flanks of Mt. Rainier.

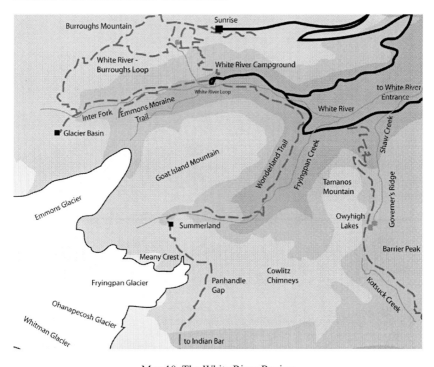

Map 10 The White River Region

147

The Owyhigh Lakes are two blue gems set in a green valley beneath the serrated cliff of Governor's Ridge. The trail is a modest climb to the lakes, which are 3.5 miles from the White River Road. This is one of the trails to the high country that is often open first and is popular in early summer.

The lakes were named for a chief of the Yakimas, whose name is usually spelled "Owhi". It is said that Owhi spent many summers in the Mt. Rainier region, especially the meadows of Sunrise.

The trailhead is just 2.2 miles inside the White River Entrance Station. As the signpost there indicates, the trail to the lakes continues on to the other side of Governor's Ridge and Barrier Peak, reaching the Eastside Highway at Deer Creek and connecting to the Eastside Trail to Ohanapecosh. In fact, the nicest part of this trail is the pass that is 1/3 mile farther on from the lakes, where there are meadows, open parkland and distant vistas.

The trail begins in a nice lowland forest on the slopes of Tamanos Mountain. Most of the route is in forest, with only occasional breaks in the cover, such as at the first switchback, where there is a view of the narrow, gravel-strewn valley of Shaw Creek. The trail gains altitude fairly quickly, but comfortably, by means of four broad switchbacks. At 5250 feet, where it begins to level off, it crosses a small tributary of Shaw Creek on a one-log bridge.

From here on the trail is more open, passing through sub-alpine forest. Soon the trail reaches the two Owyhigh Lakes. Both are surrounded by green meadows and flower fields in season. The larger lake is set neatly at the base of Governor's Ridge.

The lakes are beautifully arranged in a spectacular setting, but there's more. It would be a mistake not to continue a half mile or so farther on the trail to the high meadows and views that are found at the pass next to Barrier Peak. Flower fields of red, white and blue (paintbrush, squaw grass and lupine) greet the hiker here. The broad green slopes of Tamanos Mountain are to the north. Black bears are not infrequent in its high meadowlands.

At the top of the pass a grand view is had of the Cowlitz Chimneys, tall rock spires that present interesting challenges to rock climbers.

Summerland is one of the most popular hike destinations in the area and for good reason. The hike up to the meadows is pleasant and not too long (4.2 miles) and the reward is stupendous: high, rolling hills covered in flowers, a grand view of the mountain, and access to even higher, more arctic country. It's also an excellent place for sightings of mountain goats, which are sometimes seen scaling cliffs high above the meadows.

Although mostly in forest, the beginnings of the trip include some sunny parts. Views of Rainier are few, except for an occasional peek at its snowy slopes.

The estimated 400 foot bridges in the Park include lots of different bridge architecture. In addition to being a welcome alternative to wading across the rivers and creeks, they are usually attractive structures.

151

As the forest cover thins, the high knobs of the Panhandle Peaks come into view. The first good view of Rainier is of the steep, rocky cliffs of Willis Wall.

Until here the trail has been following Fryingpan Creek, a hundred feet or so above it to the north. Now a fairly large bridge carries hikers across the creek to its south side.

Looking down at it from the bridge in late summer, the creek looks innocent enough, but in spring its floodwaters have taken out the bridge here more than once.

Summerland is reached after a few short switchbacks.

Streams, cliffs, copses, flower fields and views of the summit of Rainier greet hikers at Summerland. There's even a small shelter, here for more than 50 years as protection for those who come in bad weather. A small number of camping sites are here for overnighters who want to witness sunrise on the mountain. Reservations are required.

Summerland is a great place to relax, to watch the goats making their way across the steep cliffs above and to make friends with the marmots.

Though nobody will claim that it's always like summer in Summerland, everyone agrees that the area above it towards Panhandle Gap is always more like winter. There is continual snow and ice there and its small lake remains frozen most of the year. This microclimate is the result of the fact that the valley below Panhandle Gap lies on the north side of the bulky ridge of Meany Crest, where it collects lots of snow in winter and is almost always in the shade in summer, so the snow never melts. (Perhaps surprisingly, Meany Crest didn't get its name by denying sun to the valley; it was named to honor Edmund Meany, University of Washington professor and well-known mountaineer of the early 20th century).

The trail to Panhandle Gap is a continuation of the Wonderland Trail beyond Summerland. It reaches one of the highest elevations anywhere on the Wonderland Trail at 6800 feet. The distance from the road below is 5.6 miles and from Summerland it's 1.4 miles.

Above Summerland the trail climbs up a rocky slope among small copses of sub-alpine firs. There are steps in steep places.

The black lava rocks give the surroundings a desolate and almost lunar look. Meany Crest looms above.

A massive log bridge crosses a stream, which in early summer is a foaming mass of melt water, but in late summer is quiet and innocent-looking, hardly in need of such a big, sturdy bridge.

The green waters of a small arctic lake come into view and snow lingers on the hillsides even in September. As the trail steepens, its path is marked by rocks lining its sides. To the west Goat Island Mountain's jagged tree line marks the elevations between 6000 and 6500 feet, above which even alpine tree species can't easily survive. Ahead, above a glacier-like permanent ice sheet, is the broad, curved pass called Panhandle Gap. The trail heads to the left to try to avoid the snow.

Looking back, Rainier is in view above the green waters of the arctic tarn.

Panhandle Gap is a wide notch in the ridge of peaks and it provides a wonderfully mountain-climber's kind of view of cliffs and snow and rocks and ice.

Day hikers with extra energy and ambition or backpackers who have reserved a camp space there can reach the magical valley of Indian Bar from the White River Road. The distance is just under 9 miles one way and there is a lot of elevation gained and lost, about 9500 feet for the round trip. The hike includes a tramp through the meadows of Summerland (Hike 59), a climb over the icy heights of Panhandle Gap (Trail 61) and a scenic descent to the enchanted valley of the upper Ohanapecosh at Indian Bar, where the river braids its way through flowery and gravelly meadows and waterfalls line the cliffs above. The entire route is on the Wonderland Trail (Hike 125).

The trail beyond Panhandle Gap seems desolate at first, as the way traverses the lower slopes of Meany Crest at the base of Little Tahoma.

As elevation is lost, the treeline is gained and the trail descends through Subalpine Firs, hemlocks and wildflowers to the valley floor, seen below in a photo taken from the ridge to the south. Indian Bar, in the lower right, is the flat graveled stream bed of the young Ohanapecosh River. The Ohanapecosh Glaciers lie above it and on the horizon are the tops of Little Tahoma and "Big Tahoma" (i.e., Mt. Rainier).

Overnighters or rain-soaked dayhikers will welcome the stone shelter at Indian Bar, a magnificent building that Betty Filley, in her wonderful book on the Wonderland Trail calls the "Wonderland Hilton". It's a grand thing to stand in front of this handsome building (or its famous outhouse) and gaze at the cliffs and waterfalls all around.

Often the Park Service will build a short trail near a campground so that campers can

have a place to walk, perhaps with small children or in the evening after a long drive and making camp. The White River Campground has such a trail, a half mile loop trip through forest and along the river. The forest here at this altitude (4200 feet) includes some lowland trees (e.g., Western Hemlocks), but mostly is made up of Intermediate Zone trees: Noble Fir, Alaska Yellow Cedar and Western White Pine. It also has deep forest flowers, such as the little orchid called Western Coralroot.

The trail descends to the river, where a few optimistic willow trees grow, oblivious of the fact that the White River often floods the valley with violent spring torrents, wiping out any vegetation. There are no trees here taller than about 10 feet.

The trail loops back through the forest to the campground.

The Emmons Glacier is Mt. Rainier's largest. It has an area of 4.3 square miles. From the summit to its present terminus is an elevation difference of over 9000 feet. It's an active

glacier with a long history of advances and retreats and floods and lahars (violent mudflows). The Emmons Moraine Trail visits the rocky edges of this giant's empire and provides a scenic lesson in glaciology. The trail begins at the White River Campground and shares its path with the Glacier Basin Trail (Hike 64) for 1.5 miles. From the junction, it's about 1.4 miles to the end of the maintained trail on the moraine's ridge.

The trail starts in forest, following for a while the route of the old road that once led to the Starbo Mine at Glacier Basin. In a few hundred yards it passes a graceful waterfall. The stream comes all the way down from Shadow Lake in Yakima Park near Sunrise (Hike 71).

Off to the left is the high ridge top of Goat Island Mountain. The stripes on its sides mark the paths of winter avalanches.

Watch for the trail sign a mile and a half from the start. The Emmons Moraine Trail descends into a small valley created by a tributary of the White River called the Inter Fork. It originates far above in the Inter Glacier, which occupies an "inter" basin between two giant glaciers, the Emmons and the Winthrop. In summer the Inter Fork is a pretty stream that bubbles its way down through a rocky bed surrounded by greenery.

The first unusual feature to see is a kettle lake, formed by glacial runoff and maintained by precipitation. Kettle lakes are usually greenish because of the rock flour they contain and they are not very permanent features, changing with the coming and going of the ice sheets that give them birth.

Rainier comes into view. In this photo the rubble of the lateral (side) moraine is in the lower right and the edge of the glacier's most recent maximum thickness is the sharp boundary at the bottom of the forest on the triangular pinnacle below Mt. Ruth. The opening of the terminus, from which the White River flows, is at lower left.

The trail continues up through scattered groves of trees.

As it comes closer to the glacier, the snout is more conspicuous. The ice is covered with debris from the slopes above, including the result of a massive landslide that brought down immense amount of rock from the upper slopes of Little Tahoma.

Looking back, the lower moraine is studded with kettle lakes, ridges of morainal debris and scattered young trees.

The official trail ends on the sharp edge of the lateral moraine, high above the current position of the active ice sheet. Although informal paths seem to go farther, it is best to turn back from here. This area is fragile and boots can quickly turn it into a network of ugly, eroded channels of dust.

Glacier Basin is a high (6400 foot) meadow located between the Emmons and Winthrop Glaciers and at the bottom of the valley formed by the Inter Glacier. You don't see any glaciers from Glacier Basin. Instead it is a scenic parkland nestled beneath high ridges and spectacular rocky cliffs.

The trail begins at the White River Campground and is 3.5 miles long (some editions of the Green Trails maps make it much longer, but this appears be an error). It follows the route of an old mining road established before the National Park was formed. The entire trail is along the scenic little river called the Inter Fork, which flows from the Inter Glacier.

The history of Glacier Basin is surprising to those who think of the national parks as being inviolate to development. Minerals, especially copper, were found here in the 1890's and mining claims were filed. The law allowed the mines to continue activity even after the establishment of the National Park in 1899. Many additional claims were filed and mining activity continued for several decades. A road was built up from Greenwater and support buildings for the mines were constructed at Glacier Basin, including a hotel, a power plant, and a sawmill. The mines were active throughout the first half of the 20th century, but never very profitable. In fact, in the 1920's two of the principles of the Mount Rainier Mining Company were convicted of mail fraud in connection with the mines and were sentenced to two years in the Federal Penitentiary on McNeil Island. In the 1940's stockholders valued the mineral deposits at more than $2 million, but independent geologists estimated their value at about $500. Mining activity was over by 1960 and the equipment and buildings are now sparsely-distributed ruins.

The trail is wide and comfortable, ascending gradually through forest, crossing many creeks coming down from Sunrise. The trail stays mostly on the slopes above the northern bank of the Inter Fork.

Mining equipment is passed along the trailside, apparently left here and there at random.

There's a trail junction about 2 ½ miles from the start; the trail to the right makes a steep but gloriously scenic ascent of Burroughs Mountain and leads on to Sunrise (Hike 65). A camp is nestled among trees near the entrance to the flat meadowlands of Glacier Basin. As one enters the meadows the view above to the right includes St. Elmo's Pass. The former route of the trail to Carbon River went over that pass and down to the side of the Winthrop Glacier on the other side of the ridge.

The trail goes on up the valley, but the higher part is mostly used by climbers intending to climb the mountain via the Emmons route. Adventurous hikers can follow the climbers' route up the rugged valley above the basin, which leads to Camp Sherman, a climbers' rough refuge where they can spend a bit of the night before their early morning trek up the glacier to the summit.

 Most day hikers are content to enjoy the meadows and views before heading back along this scenic trail.

Hike 65 – The White River-Burroughs Mountain Loop map pg. 147

Although it's fairly long (12.5 miles total) and steep in places, this loop trip is marvelously scenic and varied and worth the effort of hiking it. It starts at the White River Campground, follows the Glacier Basin Trail (Hike 64) much of its length and then switchbacks up the steep side of Burroughs Mountain to its arctic-like top. Thence it descends into the green meadows of Sunrise and finally follows the Wonderland Trail back down to White River. Of course, the trip can also be done up-side-down, beginning and ending at Sunrise.

The description of the first part, from White River towards Glacier Basin, can be found in Hikes 63 and 64. This part of the trail is wide and gentle.

The loop trip begins at an intersection that is 2 ½ miles from the parking lot at the White River campground. It passes through a grove of trees and ascends via many short switchbacks among scattered trees. Little Tahoma is conspicuous in the east, clearly from this vantage a separate volcanic mountain on its bigger sibling's flanks.

Soon the trail is in the open, where it remains until the descent to White River again. It's a view-intensive trip, with Rainier being in view for most of the time

The south slope of Burroughs is lined with flowers in season, scattered among large blocky rocks and alpine trees.

Off to the east is the White River Valley and Highway 410 in the distance. Across the valley is Goat Island Mountain. Your chances of seeing mountain goats there are better than the chances of seeing an island.

Far below are Glacier Basin and its trails.

Above the valley is Rainier, its glaciers gleaming in the sun. The triangular feature just left of center is Steamboat Prow. Camp Shurman, an overnight staging place for climbers, is located at the apex of the Prow. Willis Wall is on the right horizon and Disappointment Cleaver projects up on the far left horizon.

As contrast, the view ahead on the trail is of Burroughs Mountain's barren, tundra-like slopes.

The trail tops out at about 7400 feet on the rocky summit of Burroughs. Sluiskin Mountain appears over the horizon to the northwest.

The trail comes to an intersection near another, lower summit of Burroughs and one has to make a choice. The route to the left stays high before descending to the settlement at Sunrise. The more scenic route is to the right, which leads to spectacular Emmons Overlook. This way avoids the crowds at the road end at Sunrise.

It passes pretty Shadow Lake (Hike 71) before descending back to White River on one of the most pleasant and comfortable sections of the Wonderland Trail.

Chapter 8 - The Sunrise Region

The Sunrise Region of the Park is well-named. Set high on a flat ridgetop north of the peak, it provides a glorious view of Rainier at sunrise, with the glaciers glowing pink in the early morning light. Of course, as there are no car campgrounds or lodgings at Sunrise, only early risers from White River and backpackers at the Sunrise Camp are likely to see the sun rise on the mountain from here.

Because of its high elevation (6400 feet), the area is open for only a short while; its road is usually closed by snow until early July and after mid-October. During this time, however, thousands of people drive to see its glorious views.

Sunrise is 16 miles from the White River Entrance on a spectacular road that switchbacks its way up the side of the Sourdough Mountain Range before breaking out onto the meadows of Yakima Park (the parkland was named this long ago because of the fact that members of the Yakima Tribe were known to visit the region). The facilities there are dominated by a large parking lot. At the far end of the parking area is an excellent visitor's center that is located in a historic log building that resembles a pioneer blockhouse.

Years ago there were many more facilities here, including two car campgrounds, a lodge with a restaurant and a field full of rental cabins. The very short season, together with budget shortfalls, eventually led to the elimination of most of these conveniences. The original lower campground has been closed for many decades, now replaced by a small backpackers' camp. The upper campground is now a pleasant walk-in picnic area. The rental cabins are also long gone, though their ghosts can be seen in the upper meadows, where the scars outlining where their foundation were, are still barely visible. However, the lodge still stands next to the parking lot. Inside is a basic hamburger-style cafeteria together with a small shop.

Short trails at Sunrise explore the parkland itself, visiting its several viewpoints and its small lakes. Somewhat longer trails lead up into the Sourdough Range, including an ascent of its highest peak and of an historic lookout peak. Other, longer trails cross over the range and lead down into verdant alpine valleys to the north. And a network of trails provides access to the barren heights of Burroughs Mountain with its spectacular views of Rainier and the Winthrop and Emmons Glaciers. Finally, there is the Wonderland Trail, which passes through Sunrise on its long trek around the mountain. In spite of its short season, Sunrise is the center of many well-used hiking opportunities.

The first Sunrise trail to be encountered has its trailhead about 3 miles short of the end of the road. At a sharp switchback at Sunrise Point, there is a parking area and viewpoint. From here hikers can take a short trail to a pretty alpine lake called Sunrise Lake that lies 400 feet almost directly below the point.

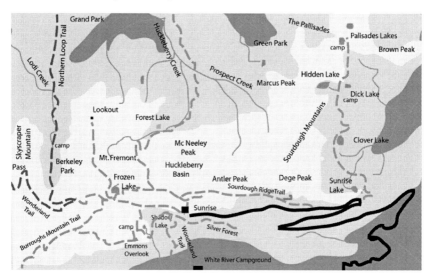

Map 11 Sunrise Region

The trailhead is well-marked just to the east of the parking area, where there is a sign and exhibit. The trail to Sunrise Lake heads down almost immediately and reaches the lake in about 0.6 miles. About a half mile from the start the trail divides. To the right is the continuation of the trail to several other, more distant lakes (Hikes 67 and 68). The branch to the left leads to the shore of Sunrise Lake.

The lake is located at the south end of a large meadowland called White River Park, which occupies a rather flat area of sub-alpine woods, grassy fields and lakes below the rocky slopes of the Sourdough Range. From the top of that range, Sunrise Lake appears as a blue jewel set in a bowl of trees and meadows.

For a gratifying trip through high woods and meadows that passes several beautiful lakes, it would be hard to beat the trail to Palisades Lakes. On its way to its end at Upper Palisades Lake, the trail, 3.5 miles long, passes close to seven mountain lakes (one, Hidden Lake, requires a detour up a spur trail, described as Hike 68). Views are of parklands and cliffs and distant mountains to the north, but not of Mt. Rainier, which is largely obscured by the Sourdough Mountain Range.

The trailhead is at Sunrise Point, described for Hike 66. The first part of the trail is in common with the trail to Sunrise Lake, going northeast from the road and swiftly down. The view to the north is of Marcus Peak (left) and Palisades Peak.

The trail most of the way is comfortable, soft and, except for a couple of ups and downs, relatively level.

The trail tends to stay in the open, passing among the clumps of sub-alpine trees. In early summer the meadows are studded with flowers, in late summer there are delicious low-bush blueberries to eat and in the autumn the blueberry fields become crimson with fall color.

Having passed close to Sunrise Lake near the start of the trip, the trail comes to its second lake, large, meadow-fringed Clover Lake, 1½ miles from the trailhead.

From the lake the trail goes up and over a low ridge. There follows a section that is picturesquely made up of meadows punctuated by large white boulders.

A trail junction is at 2½ miles. The branch trail to the left leads up to Hidden Lake (Hike 68). In another 1/3 mile the trail comes to Dick's Lake.

The lake is one of three forest-fringed small lakes, commonly known as Tom, Dick and Harry Lakes. There is a small backcountry camp at Dick's Lake. While Tom Lake, though nearby, is out of view from the trail, Harry Lake is passed to the right and below the trail shortly after Dick's Lake.

You know that you are getting close to the Palisades Lakes when the Palisades themselves come into view to the left. The columnar cliffs on the mountain receive their name from their stake-like sharp, vertical shape.

The last half mile of trail crosses a large open meadow between the Palisades and Brown Peak. There are views of the more distant mountains off to the north. The end of the trail is at the two Palisades Lakes. Lower Palisades Lake can be seen off to the right. It lies 350 feet lower than its sibling. There is no trail down to its remote shores.

The Upper Palisades Lake is especially beautiful, lying at the base of the Palisades Cliffs. For those so-prepared, it is possible to camp overnight at Upper Palisades Lake (permits are required). The camp area is reached on a spur trail that goes to the left and up the side of the slopes above the lake.

A side trail from the Palisades Lakes Trail (Hike 67), about 2.6 miles from its trailhead, leads to a hidden lake called, reasonably enough, Hidden Lake. Of course, it's no longer hidden very well, as the trail is well-marked and frequently taken. The trail distance from the main trail is about a half mile and there is about 300 feet of elevation gain.

The high meadows near the lake are largely a mix of flowers and low bush blueberries. At these elevations (5900 feet), meadowlands are extremely fragile and the Hidden Lake meadows are an excellent example. Boots in the past destroyed them when hikers scattered here and there, not sticking to a well-established single trail. In the late 90's the Park Service brought netting, soil, new plants and signs to the meadows to attempt to restore them. They are coming back.

The lake is exceptionally nicely set among these meadows and dwarf trees.

It lies in a nearly perfectly circular glacial cirque, with rocky cliffs towering above on nearly all sides.

After getting out of their cars and making a quick visit to the restrooms and the handsome visitor center at Sunrise, most visitors are attracted to the trail that rises up from the parking area to the north. Large signs with maps explain the many destinations reached from this trailhead, the most popular being a loop trip up into the Sourdough Range that follows a self-guiding route for which there are guide booklets available (usually) at the trailhead. This nature trail is 1.5 miles long and it provides a mini-course in sub-alpine ecology with its 13 signed stops.

But the loop trip is just a short part of the Sourdough Ridge trail system. The main trail up the slope divides at the top. The trail to the left (west) goes to Frozen Lake (Hike 75), Mt. Fremont Lookout (Hike 76) and farther destinations. The trail to the right (east) goes along the ridge of the Sourdough Mountains Range, with a side trail to the summit of Dege Peak (Hike 70). The ridge trail finally ends near the parking area at Sunrise Point, 3 miles from the trailhead and 300 feet lower in elevation than the start.

To reach the Ridge Trail, one takes the wide path that leaves the parking lot just to the left of the lodge building, where the restaurant and shop are now located (it formally was the center of overnight accommodations, which included over 200 rustic cabins). In a few hundred yards the trail divides. Going right will take you east along the Sourdough Ridge.

The Sourdough Mountain Range is about 10 miles long and includes a series of peaks topping at just over 7000 feet high. The first named mountain encountered on this trail is 7017 foot high Antler Peak, a sharp prominence that the trail skirts just under on the south, seen here from the trail beyond it near Dege Peak.

From the saddles between peaks views to the north open up spectacularly. White River Park is spread out below beneath the northern Sourdough Mountains, including Marcus (left) and Brown Peaks.

Even more distant mountains can be recognized on the horizon, including the prominent peak of Mt. Stuart, 50 miles to the northeast. The altitude gained on this trail also brings many mountains into view to the south. The most prominent, of course, is Mt. Rainier.

Below the trail is the Sunrise Road and just beyond it is the shelf of high meadow lands that make up the eastern end of Yakima Park.

Hike 70 – Dege Peak map pg. 172

A short side trail from the Sourdough Ridge Trail (Hike 69) allows the ascent of Dege Peak. As mountain climbs go, this is especially easy. The trail is wide and gentle and the distance is only 0.3 miles. But the reward is as fine as those of more strenuous mountain ascents, with marvelous, unobstructed views of the surroundings in all directions. The Dege Peak Trail leaves the Sourdough Ridge Trail 1.4 miles from Sunrise.

The summit of Dege is steep on the north and more gradual on the south, where the trail ascends.

The trail proceeds upwards through groves of subalpine forest, clumps of flowers, especially lupine and asters, and volcanic rock.

Near the top the trail turns to the right, reaches a flat rocky platform of a summit and the views open up all around. To the west are the rugged peaks of the Sourdough Range to the northwest is the huge, flat, green meadow of Grand Park.

Below in the north is the small, charming parkland at the headwaters of Prospector Creek, with Marcus Peak rising above it to the right.

Just east of the Sourdough Range ridgeline is another green meadowland, White River Park, with peaceful, blue Clover Lake at its center.

To the east is Sunrise Lake, nestled under Sunrise Ridge. The trail to the lake and the parking area at Sunrise Point are just visible.

The tooth-like pinnacles of Governor's Ridge are to the south. Barrier Peak is the broader peak attached to the Ridge to the right, while Tamanos Mountain is closer and farther to the right.

Directly south are the Cowltiz Chimneys. The Sarvent Glaciers lie below their summits and Fryingpan Creek is visible far below them.

Among the several short trails available from the Sunrise parking lot, one of the pleasantest is the 1.2 mile trail to Shadow Lake, a quiet mountain pond in the meadows of Yakima Park. The trail leaves the parking lot near the visitor center and divides shortly after leaving the pavement. The left branch goes to Emmons Vista (Hike 73); take the right branch, which leads to Shadow Lake. After a half mile of wandering through beautiful meadows and scattered subalpine trees, the trail joins the Wonderland Trail. To the left the Wonderland begins its descent to White River and to the right it leads to the lake. There is a brief ascent over a low ridge before the trail crosses a couple of small creeks and passes alongside a large, smooth meadow.

The trail then enters a wooded area surrounding Shadow Lake. There is a trail that traverses up above the side of the lake and loops around to return to the main trail to the west, with steps down to the lake shore. The outlet of the lake has a few silver logs arranged in the shallows.

This part of the Park is undergoing extensive rehabilitation. Many years ago there was a campground near Shadow Lake, reached by a gravel road from upper Sunrise, and overuse badly damaged the meadows. The Park has returned much of the campground area and the road to their natural state. A hikers' camp is located just beyond the lake, but that is all that remains from the days when these meadows were crowded with cars and trailers and tents and lots of people.

The trail goes on to spectacular Emmons Overlook (Hike 72) and Burroughs Mountain (Hike 77). To get a better idea of the layout of this part of Yakima Park, take the Sourdough Ridge Trail (Hike 69), which gives an excellent view of Shadow Lake and its surroundings.

The Emmons Glacier is Mt. Rainier's largest. A nice trail to a spectacular view of this huge sheet of ice is available from Sunrise. The distance from the Sunrise visitor center is 1.5 miles and the first part of the trail is the same as that followed to Shadow Lake (see Hike 71 for directions). From the lake, the route heads south about 0.3 miles up the slopes of Burroughs Mountain to the Overlook, which is perched on the edge of a steep cliff, providing an uninterrupted view of the glacier.

The trail passes through Sunrise Camp, a place where backpackers can camp overnight. The site is what is left of a former car campground, decommissioned over 50 years ago. The camp spots are pleasantly scattered among the trees, there is an outhouse, and hidden in the trees is the ruins of one of the restrooms of the former campground.

The trail to Emmons Overlook leaves the camp's western edge and begins traversing up the slope of Burroughs Mountain.

The Overlook is located at a sharp, hairpin turn in the trail, where there is a handsome stone wall and space to stop and rest.

Gazing at the mountain from here, one is looking at the north face of Rainier, its iciest side, where almost all of the upper mountain is glacier-covered. Peering over the wall, one gets an excellent view of the terminus of the Emmons Glacier, so covered with debris that it looks more like gray dirt than rock-covered ice.

Directly below the Overlook is the valley of the glacier's outflow, the White River. Bright green lakes, colored by whitish glacial dust in suspension, dot the valley floor.

The Emmons Glacier is immense, reaching from the mountain's summit down some 9000 feet in elevation to its terminus, and spreading out over more than four square miles. It is marked by ice falls and crevasses as it flows slowly down over the irregular icebed of the mountain.

A tamer trip to view the mighty Emmons Glacier than the hike to Emmons Overlook (Hike 72) is provided by the Emmons Vista Trail. A wonderful view of the glacier and its mountain is reached on a wide trail only 0.3 miles long. From the Sunrise parking lot take the trail that leaves southward just east of the visitor center. At the trail junction, turn left along the Rim Trail. A short trail section leads south to the Vista. The path leads through fine examples of subalpine parkland and often has deer and (sometimes elk) grazing among the groves of Subalpine Fir.

A treasure of this short hike, besides the vista itself, is the sign that points the way down to the viewing platform. It's one of the few classical wooden National Park Signs left. It is a wide, brown-painted wooden sign with an arrowhead pointing the way instead of an arrow. In place in 2003, it may give way to the modern metal signs in the future. Some of us, who have been visiting the national parks for many decades, hope that it can stay as a sort of a mini historical exhibit.

It's only a few steps down to the Vista platform, perched strategically above the valley. From here the view encompasses the entire length of the Emmons Glacier from its beginnings at Columbia Crest to its end in the rocky moraine, where the White River carries its milky meltwater on down towards Puget Sound.

A hike to an interesting example of a "ghost forest" is another of the short trips possible from Sunrise. To find the Silver Forest Trail, take the access trail found just east of the Sunrise Visitors' Center. After traveling through the meadow for a few hundred yards, you'll encounter the following sign directing you to the left.

The trail has a few ups and downs but is mostly level. It soon passes the Emmons Vista turnoff (Hike 73) and wanders through patches of trees and dry volcanic meadowlands. It then enters the Silver Forest. Years ago a forest fire swept up the ridge from below, killing most of the trees on this part of the ridge. The dead trees were gradually bleached by the summer sun to a silvery, white color. Some lie on the ground but others are still standing. The trail makes its way through a gentle meadow among the white ghost forest and the on hillside to the east are more of the silver trees, now being overtaken by new trees making a new forest.

The trail officially ends at about 1.5 miles, but an unmaintained path continues on towards a pretty meadow at the end of the ridge.

The ghost trees of Silver Forest are well worth the trip, but the other reason for making it is the wide expanse of views one gets from the trail along the ridge. The White River lies below in deep forest and there are excellent views of triangularly-peaked Tamanos Mountain, with the pinnacles of Governor's Ridge beyond it to the left.

The trip to Frozen Lake is a pleasant and easy hike from Sunrise. It is on a view-intensive portion of the Sourdough Ridge Trail's (Hike 69) western branch. The lake is 1.4 miles from the Sunrise parking lot and is reached by taking the Ridge Trail upslope to the north and branching off to the left. Soon the hiker can look back at the Sunrise Complex from the heights of the ridge.

About a mile from the start the trail traverses a steep slope below one of the unnamed Sourdough peaks, where there's a rock wall formed to shore up the trail. Views of Rainier from along here are excellent.

Frozen Lake is a source of water for Sunrise, so cannot be approached closely. It's often still ice-covered in summer and patches of snow are usually there even in the autumn.

From here there are trails on to other destinations west, including to Burroughs Mountain (Hike 77) on a trail visible in this photograph.

The circle of lookouts around Mt. Rainier was established long ago for fire detection. With the advent of air patrols and satellite surveillance, they are no longer needed for that purpose, but many of them are still in place and serve as attractive goals for hikers seeking a spectacular viewpoint. In the east there's Shriner Peak (Hike 45), in the west, Gobbler's Knob (Hike 109), in the northwest, Tolmie Peak (Hike 104) and here in the north near Sunrise there's Mt. Fremont.

Mt. Fremont is a rocky peak, 7181 feet in elevation and at the western end of the Sourdough Range. The views from its top are exceptional, taking in the lush valleys of Berkeley Park and Huckleberry Creek below, the remarkable plateau of Grand Park in the north and surrounding mountains, near and far. The trail is a moderately gentle 2.7 miles, all of it in the open for continuous views. It begins at the Sunrise parking lot, leaving upwards to the north to the Sourdough Ridge Trail. The route begins identically to that for Frozen Lake (Hike 75), turning left onto the Sourdough Ridge Trail above Sunrise.

The trail turns left near Frozen Lake and ascends a hill to bypass it on the south. The Mt. Fremont Trail's route can be clearly seen from here above Frozen Lake. Just beyond the lake are some trail junctions. The trail to the left is the Wonderland Trail, which heads steeply down towards Sunrise Camp. Straight ahead are the west-bound Wonderland Trail and a junction with the Burroughs Mountain Trail. The trail to the right goes to the Fremont Lookout.

At first the trail sets off across a nearly level, nearly barren plain.

It then angles up the western slopes of the mountain, passing through low-lying patches of Sub-alpine Fir. The Bonsai-like trees are dwarfed by the harsh mountain climate.

With no trees to obscure the view the panorama is extensive. To the west is the green hollow that encompasses Berkeley Park. Above it is Skyscraper Ridge, with the pointed summit of Skyscraper Mountain at the far right. Beyond are the northwestern flanks of Rainier with Observation Rock and Echo Rock as prominent features near the center of the view.

At an altitude of just under 7000 feet the trail swings right around the shoulder of one of Mt. Fremont's several summits. From here on the trail is nearly level, dipping now and then as it traverses along the western slopes of the mountain. The lookout building, nearly a mile away still, is visible for the first time.

On a clear day the view far to the west includes the entire Olympic Mountain Range. Sluiskin Mountain and the West Fork White River Valley are in the foreground. The trail briefly sweeps around the ridge to the east side before abruptly arriving at the lookout, which is a glass-lined room above a set of stairs with a surrounding balcony.

Of course the views are fabulous from here. Mt. Rainier dominates the south.

Below the lookout, beneath the pointed top of Skyscraper Mountain, is the green valley of Berkeley Park.

Hike 77 – Burroughs Mountain map pg. 172

Burroughs Mountain is the massive hunk of rock and pumice that rises above Sunrise to the southwest. From below it looks like a desolate peak, with only faint shadings of green to soften its black and reddish volcanic surface. The presence of only minimal vegetation is the result of the harsh and very long winter and the fact that the ground, made up of porous volcanic rock, holds moisture poorly, so that plants go from being buried under snow for 10 months of the year to 2 months of drought.

A trip up onto Burroughs has some of the attributes of a trek through an arctic wilderness. But in addition to experiencing the unique, bleak environment found above timberline, the Burroughs hiker also gets some fabulous views of the glaciers below. The mountain extends a good three miles in towards the heights of Mt. Rainier, providing bird's-eye views of both the Emmons and the Winthrop Glaciers, the mountain's two largest.

Burroughs Mountain has a roughly flat top at an elevation of around 7000 feet. There are three high points, called First, Second and Third Burroughs. The last of these is the highest, at 7828 feet, and it is the one with the most spectacular glacier view, as one looks almost straight down at the Winthrop Glacier.

There are several ways to ascend Burroughs Mountain by trail. The following describes a very scenic loop trip (with an extension), but one may choose other routes by planning from a Sunrise area map. We choose a counterclockwise loop, as it provides the most spectacular views of Rainier from the ascent. The loop trip plus extension totals about 6 miles.

Begin at the Sunrise parking lot and head upslope from near the Lodge towards the Sourdough Ridge Trail (Hike 69). Turn left on the Ridge Trail and continue to Frozen Lake (Hike 75), just beyond which is a trail junction. Turn left onto the Burroughs Mountain Trail. This trail heads up the steep north slopes of Burroughs and often has snow covering it even in August. These snow patches can be dangerous, so proceed with caution.

A half mile from Frozen Lake the trail levels off. Turning back, you'll have a view of the lake and of one of the summits of Mt. Fremont beyond it. This portion of the trail has views mostly to the north. As the trail gets higher the northern terrain of the Park becomes spread out like a map. It is even possible to make out some of the trails that carry hikers west from Sunrise, to such destinations as the Mt. Fremont Lookout (Hike 76), Berkeley Park (Hike 79), Skyscraper Mountain (Hike 83) and the distant valley of the White River's West Fork.

As the trip ascends above Frozen Lake, the Wonderland Trail is visible below as it winds its way up to the pass to the left of Skyscraper Mountain. Beyond is sharp pillared Sluiskin Mountain.

Nearing the first summit, the tundra extends gently off to the north. Skyscraper Mountain is beyond.

A trail junction about 2½ miles from the start is near the First Burroughs summit. In these high parts of the mountain the trail is wide and sandy with rocks marking its boundaries. Hikers should stay on the trails, as the few plants that can survive in this harsh environment easily can be killed by a single boot step.

From the trail junction at First Burroughs, one can turn left and return to Sunrise via the scenic Emmons Overlook route (Hike 72). For more high country adventure, however, one can continue straight ahead to Second Burroughs, where the trail from Glacier Basin reaches its high point (Hike 65). Although there is no official trail to Third Burroughs, a boot path leads there, where the view down to the Winthrop Glacier is superb.

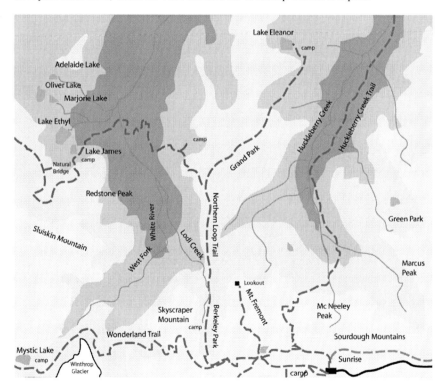

Map 12 Sunrise West and North

Hike 78 – The Northern Loop

map pg. 204

The Northern Loop trail trip is a backpacking route through some of the more remote country in the Park. A two or three day adventure, it is 18.3 miles in length and it involves a lot of spectacular ups and downs. One can go either clockwise or counterclockwise and can start either at Sunrise or at Carbon River. This description takes the counterclockwise direction, departing from Sunrise.

Begin by reserving space at the backcountry camps where you wish to stay. There are (usually) eight choices: Berkeley Park, Fire Creek, Redstone, Yellowstone Cliffs, Carbon River, Dick Creek, Mystic Lake and Granite Creek. A fairly comfortable three-day trip can be made with overnight stops at Redstone near Lake James and Mystic Lake, but other choices are also possible. When you reserve your space you will learn which camps are open at that time.

The trip begins by heading up to the Sourdough Trail from the Sunrise parking lot. Turn left at the top and follow the route described for Hike 75 to Frozen Lake. At the trail intersection, continue on west on the Wonderland Trail for about ¾ mile to a junction. The Northern Loop trip leaves the Wonderland Trail here, taking the path to the right towards Berkeley Park (Hike 79) and Grand Park (Hike 80). The Berkeley Park Camp is 2.3 miles beyond the Frozen Lake intersection and Grand Park is entered after another scenic 2 miles. But one hardly has a chance to enjoy Grand Park's magnificent grandeur before there's a trail junction, with the Northern Loop Trail turning off to the left, dropping away from Grand Park into the West Fork Valley of the White River.

The trail descends steeply into the valley via many switchbacks, encountering the turnoff for Fire Creek Camp about half way down. Having descended to the river by means of some 40 or more switchbacks, the trail then ascends from the river by another 40 switchbacks to Lake James and the Redstone backcountry camp.

We were unable to obtain close-up photographs of Lakes James and Ethel because when we headed there in 2003, the trail was closed because of a forest fire. In this view from Mt. Fremont, taken in 2004, one can see the two lakes nestled in the forest. The burned-out forest is on the ridge in the left foreground.

From Lake James the Northern Loop Trail ascends up along the valley of van Horn Creek, passing a spur trail to a patrol cabin along the way. About a mile and a half from Lake James the trail crests at Windy Gap (Hike 94), an attractive meadow area below the spires of Sluiskin Mountain.

For the remainder of this trip, the trails are described elsewhere: between Windy Gap and Carbon River (Hike 94) between Carbon River and Moraine Park (Hike 93) and the rest of the way back to Sunrise on the Wonderland Trail (Hike 125).

There are many alpine parklands near timberline around Mt. Rainier and each has its own special characteristics. Berkeley Park is a fine example. It has two personalities, both attractive. Upper Berkeley Park is a dry, treeless arctic garden, with tufts of flowers spread out among the fields of frothy volcanic pebbles. Lower Berkeley Park, in contrast, is a lush green valley with a cheerful stream winding its way through grassy meadows and clumps of trees.

Reaching this park from Sunrise involves a scenic 3.8 mile trail trip. First head north upslope from Sunrise Lodge to the Sourdough Ridge Trail (Hike 69). Turn left and follow that trail to Frozen Lake (Hike 75). Continue on the Wonderland Trail west about ¾ of a mile past the lake to an intersection. The trail to the right leaves the Wonderland Trail to descend into the Berkeley Basin to Berkeley Park and farther destinations. The wider trail to the left continues west, gradually ascending to Skyscraper Pass and on around the mountain.

Upper Berkeley Park's sunny slopes are graced with flowers in the summer and red and tawny fall colors in the autumn. A few hardy sub-alpine trees, no taller than shrubs, cling to the porous soil.

Looking down into lower Berkeley Park, one sees a different environment, with green meadows and clumps of larger trees. Off to the north are the deep forests of the northern, remote regions of Rainer National Park and the distant Cascades beyond. Berkeley Park is protected on the west by Skyscraper Mountain and on the east by slightly higher Mt. Fremont.

Lodi Creek, said to have been named by early prospectors, wanders through the valley. Pink monkey flowers and white bistort line its rocky banks. Berkeley Park Camp is hidden in the trees near the creek. Giant boulders, fallen from Mt. Fremont, line the eastern side of the valley.

On the west the steep slopes of Skyscraper Mountain rise above the meadows.

Appropriately-named Grand Park is a remarkable meadow, nearly flat, almost treeless and over a square mile in area. It's the top of an old sheet of volcanic ash and pumice, eroded away on all sides so that it sits like a table top above its surroundings. If it were chopped off and hauled down to Arizona, folks would call it a mesa.

Grand Park is reached from Sunrise in about 6½ miles of scenic trail travel. The trip is not especially strenuous and the destination is so amazing that it is well worth hiking the longish distance. The route is the same as followed for Berkeley Park (Hike 79); one heads up to the Sourdough Trail from Sunrise, turns left and hikes to Frozen Lake and follows the Wonderland Trail to the Northern Loop, Berkeley Park junction. After heading down into cozy Berkeley Park, the trail continues on another 3 miles to Grand Park.

Below Berkeley Park the trail reaches a forested saddle. Cliffs below the saddle frame the view down to the west into the valley of the West Fork.

The trail reaches a low point at 5400 feet and then begins a gentle climb to Grand Park. Looking back past the tufts of beargrass and the stately alpine trees, the view of Rainier is dominated by the mile-wide cliff of Willis Wall.

The trail approaches the flat plateau of Grand Park from its left side, skirting its southern edge as it ascends gently through the thinning stands of trees.

Finally, at an elevation of 5600 feet, the park is reached. The trail crosses along its western boundary, continuing a mile and a half, the full length of this remarkable meadow. It's worth it to continue at least part of the way across the park, especially so as to get a good view back to Rainier with the expanse of Grand Park in the foreground.

A pleasant destination from Sunrise is this quiet, small lake located deep in the valley north of Mt. Fremont. It is 2.5 easy miles from the Sunrise parking lot and most of the trail is in the open, with views first to the south to Rainier and later to the north to parklands and distant Cascades.

The trip begins by ascending the wide trail upslope from near Sunrise Lodge to join the Sourdough Ridge Trail (Hike 69). Turning left on this popular trail brings you to a trail junction a little over ½ miles from the start. Turn right to begin the descent into the valley of Huckleberry Creek. The trail junction is at an elevation of 6800 feet and the lake is down at 5650 feet, so be prepared for a pleasant descent but a more strenuous return.

The Huckleberry Creek Trail continues on all the way to the northern border of the National Park, about 10 miles from Sunrise (Hike 82).

Views from the top of the trail are first of Mt. Fremont, rising ahead above the sandy trail. The lookout is on a more distant summit, hidden behind these rocky heights.

The view east is of Huckleberry Basin and the eastern Sourdough Mountains. A series of switchbacks brings the trail down to the right towards a pointed peak. The trail then heads to the left into a rocky basin.

Far below is the valley, with the trail just visible as it meanders across the meadow. Hidden in the forest to the left of the meadow is appropriately-named Forest Lake.

Soon the meadow is reached. It is mostly a grassy meadow with small sub-alpine trees scattered across it. The trail crosses the west fork of Huckleberry Creek just before both trail and creek enter the forest. A few hundreds yards more and the trail reaches Forest Lake.

It is a small lake, but usually quiet, as relatively few hikers venture down this way. There is a small campsite in the trees near the lake.

A trip on the Huckleberry Creek Trail is a long and lonesome one, passing through a quiet and isolated section of the Park that sees few visitors. It is a rewarding trail because of the variety of country traveled, from the arctic-like tundra at its high point (near 6800 feet) to the lush forest at its low point (near 3100 feet).

About 10 miles in length, the Huckleberry Creek Trail does not make a good one-day round trip except for exceptionally fit and ambitious hikers. Most users will probably want to break the trip into two days or will arrange to have transportation at the far end so as to do the hike one way in one day. Whether one way or round trip, the voyage can be started at either end, either at the top, where the trailhead is at the Sunrise parking lot, or at the bottom, where the trailhead is a mile outside the Park boundary in the Snoqualmie National Forest at FS Road 73. The trail is steep in places and many one-way hikers decide to go down it rather than up. On the other hand, the upward trip has the advantage of saving the glorious views and high meadows as a reward for the end of the day. This description begins at the bottom.

To reach the lower trailhead, turn right off of Highway 410 onto FS 73, about 5 ½ miles south of the settlement of Greenwater. Proceed on this gravel road just over 5 miles to a bridge that crosses over Huckleberry Creek. The trail is located on the left side of the creek and probably will not be signed, though it's obvious where it crosses a clearing below the road and heads into the trees.

Along most of the trip the creek is never far. Its murmurings and occasional louder waterfalls are a pleasant companion to an otherwise lonely journey.

About a mile from the start the trail enters the National Park. Not far beyond the boundary is a log patrol cabin, in fairly good repair in spite of not being used most of the time. On our last trip here, however, there were signs of use and voices barely heard from the direction of the creek. Investigation showed that a group of Park naturalists were staying here while making an inventory of the fish and other occupants of the creek

The next few miles are through more forest, with the trees and undergrowth very slowly changing as altitude is gained. The trail is gradual at first, remaining to the east of the creek and with its steepness matching that of the creek.

Beginning at about 4500 feet the trail steepens as it climbs up towards Huckleberry Basin. Openings in the forest begin to promise more distant views.

After passing some nice waterfalls, the trail ascends into the high country. Huckleberry Creek here is an infant compared to the robust stream of the lower valley. A simple log bridge suffices to cross it.

At last the meadows of Huckleberry Basin are reached. The sunshine (or, of course, rain) and meadow flowers provide a dramatic change from the miles of deep forest.

From the meadowland the trail ascends up into the rocky basin towards the pass between this valley and Yakima Park. The last couple of miles to Sunrise follow the route described for Forest Lake (Hike 81).

Skyscraper Mountain has formidable cliffs on its east side, making it well-named for its vertical steepness. Experienced mountain climbers upon seeing those cliffs will instantly start looking for the best routes up through cracks and chimneys. This description is not for those people. Around on the other side of Skyscraper is a gentle path (not an official trail but easily found) that comfortably leads to the summit and to the remarkable views from the top of this rocky peak.

To reach Skyscraper Mountain, one follows the Wonderland Trail west from Sunrise. The shortest route from the Sunrise parking lot is via Sourdough Ridge (Hike 69) and Frozen Lake (Hike 75), although one can also join the Wonderland via Shadow Lake and Sunrise Camp (Hike 71). From Frozen Lake the Wonderland Trail heads west to Skyscraper Pass, where the path to the peak turns off to the right. The total distance from Sunrise to the pass is 3.3 miles and the added distance up to the summit is a little less than ½ mile.

Throughout this part of the Park the soil is made up largely of pumice, which is highly porous. It does not hold water well so that vegetation has a tough time during the brief dry periods of summer. It's extremely important to stay on the trail so as not to damage the delicate existence of the mountain flowers and shrubs. This is especially true for any travel beyond official trails. Place your boots carefully, on rocks, between plants or on an existing path.

From near Frozen Lake to the west is a particularly good view of Skyscraper Mountain, which rises above the flat meadowland of upper Berkeley Park.

About 0.7 miles west of Frozen Lake the trail crosses the headwaters of tiny Lodi Creek. There is a trail junction here. The right-hand trail descends into Berkeley Park and points north. Take the left-hand trail, which is the main Wonderland Trail, which traverses the slopes of Burroughs Mountain above Berkeley Park. It descends a little into the upper part of this extensive meadowland before gradually heading upward again towards the pass.

At the pass find the well-used but unsigned path to the right. It travels gently up the west side of Skyscraper to its 7078 foot high summit. From here the views are superb in all directions. Rainier dominates the south, with the bumpy peaks of Burroughs and the long sweep of the Winthrop Glacier in the foreground. To the north is the deep valley of the West Fork of the White River and east of it the broad flat meadow of Grand Park. The northwest is dominated by the mountains towards the Carbon River valley: sharp-sided Sluiskin Mountain and Old Desolate, with nearly-inaccessible Vernal Park between them.

Below the summit is Skyscraper Pass with the Wonderland Trail visible where it begins its long descent to the snout of the Winthrop Glacier.

Mystic Lake, one of the Park's prettiest lakes, is a long day's round trip from Sunrise and therefore many visitors decide to make it a backpack destination. The one-way distance from the Sunrise parking lot is 8.7 miles. Mystic Lake also can be reached from the Carbon River road. It's a slightly shorter distance, 7.8 miles from Ipsut Creek on the Wonderland Trail.

From Sunrise, follow the trail described for Hike 83 to Skyscraper Pass. The Wonderland Trail crosses above Berkeley Park up to the pass

The way then turns downward, descending along a ridge above Winthrop Valley. Long switchbacks lead down into the Granite Creek watershed and a forested area. Thence a steep section drops lower into the lateral moraine of the Winthrop Glacier. Turning north, the trail sidesteps along the glacier to a crossing of Winthrop Creek below the glacier's terminus. Young trees grow where ice only recently covered these slopes.

The trail goes up again, first along the West Fork of the White River and then more steeply up the ridge to a basin that lies between the peaks of Old Desolate and Mineral Mountain. In the middle of this basin is beautiful Mystic Lake.

There is a backcountry camp near the lake. It's a popular destination, so be sure to reserve a space early if you plan to overnight here.

Lake Eleanor is a quiet lake in the forest near the northern boundary of the Park. It can be reached in two ways. The long way is by trail from Sunrise. One takes the Grand Park trail (Hike 80) and just keeps on going another 3 miles from the middle of Grand Park. The lake is reached in about 10 miles from Sunrise. The trail through Grand Park continues to the forest and then descends to a stream and small meadow before heading up gently among the trees, circling around a ridge to the lake.

A shorter trip can be made by entering the Park from the north via an informal trail from Forest Service Road 73. The unmarked trail leaves from near the bridge over Eleanor Creek. The distance from that gravel road is about a mile. It passes trough a nice forest, never far from Eleanor Creek. This trail is not sanctioned by the Park Service and eventually may be closed.

There is a small backcountry camp at the lake, which is surrounded by forest.

Chapter 9 - The Carbon River Region

The fourth and least know entrance to Mt. Rainier National Park is at its northwest corner, following the Carbon River valley. The road from the north passes through several interesting and historical towns: Buckley (famous for its orchard nursery), Carbonado (named for the coal mines that formerly supported the state with fuel) and Wilkenson (another former coal mining town with several elegant old buildings.

The road towards the Park actually divides just outside the boundary, providing a choice of destinations. To the right at the intersection is a gravel road that heads southeast and ends at Mowich Lake (Chapter 10). The road straight ahead continues along the Carbon River to an entrance and a ranger station at the corner of the Park. The road continues another 5 miles into the Park, ending in the deep forest at Ipsut Creek Campground. This last portion of the road is subject to damaging floods and there have been years when the road was closed to vehicles throughout the summer. It's wise to check on its condition before heading that way.

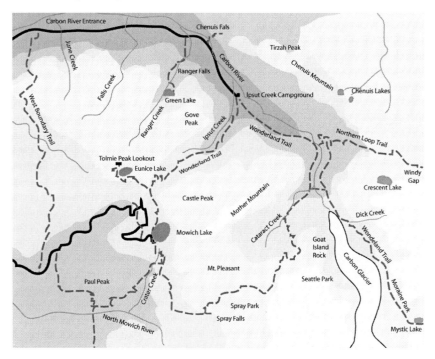

Map 13 Carbon River and Mowich Lake Regions

The first trail encountered upon entering the Park has its trailhead right at the entrance station. It is part of the system of boundary trails that once nearly encircled the Park near its boundaries. Most of these trails are now abandoned and nearly impossible to find. The West Boundary Trail near the Carbon River Entrance is an exception. It is not a maintained trail, but it can be followed (with care) over much of its 9 mile length to its end at the Mowich Lake road to the south. It follows the country's contours to some extent, which means that sometimes it's in the Park and sometimes it's across the border. Often the transition is especially noticeable when you find yourself emerging from deep, virgin forest to a barren clearcut.

This trail is included for completeness, but this book does not recommend it. It is seldom traveled, it's unmaintained and it provides little in the way of views to make up for the risk of losing the trail and becoming lost in lonely terrain. Occasionally climbers take it to gain access to minor peaks, such as forested Sweet Peak and meadow-covered Florence Peak. Hikers with good navigational skills, good topographic maps, a GPS receiver and a good compass might enjoy the experience of traveling this trail through the lonely edge of the Park, passing through portions of fine forest.

The northern trailhead is an unwelcoming sign off of the June Creek Nature Trail (Hike 87), stating that the trail in not maintained.

The southern trailhead is on the Mowich Lake road near the Mowich Lake entrance. It is difficult to find, as there is no sign at the former trailhead. To begin at that end, drive a short distance past the "Entering Mt. Rainier National Park" sign and stop near the sign that says "turn lights on for safety". The trail begins 20 yards beyond that sign on the left side of the road, just near the curve in this picture.

Once located, the trail is fairly easy to follow for about a mile north from the road. It passes through some nice forest, gaining elevation gradually.

Where it comes near to the edge of the National Park the darkness of the virgin forest fades as the bright sun from the nearby clearcut penetrates into the trees. However, after a mile or so the trail degenerates into a vagueness that could easily be troublesome. The trail is interesting, perhaps, from the historical point of view, but hikers to this part of the Park wanting a good forest hike would be much wiser to choose the nearby Paul Peak Trail (Hike 100).

Hike 87 – The June Creek Nature Trail

map pg. 224

A fine example of a short but rewarding nature trail is located right at the Carbon River entrance. The trailhead is located between the entrance station and the restrooms and there are usually some leaflets available there to guide walkers through the 0.3 mile trail and its several marked stops.

This part of the forest is an example of an inland rain forest and the trail emphasizes the unique character of such a forest. Its low elevation means that the forest is relatively warm, but the surrounding mountains mean that it is kept wet by the precipitation they cause; the combination of warmth and abundant water leads to the special features that make a rain forest. Although not as extreme as coastal rain forests like that on the west side of the Olympic Mountains, this is a fine example of an inland rain forest. Characteristic dominant undergrowth includes moss and many ferns of various kinds, including sword ferns and deer ferns. Watch also for delicate maidenhair ferns along the creek beds.

The trail crosses June Creek on a rustic bridge. This stream has its headwaters high above to the south on Florence Peak. The surroundings here are swampy, with water-saturated ground keeping the vegetation well watered all summer. The darkness of this thick forest means that the primary trees here are Western Hemlocks, which can thrive in such deep shade. The path also encounters other conifers as it progresses, including Douglas Fir, Western Red Cedar and Sitka Spruce. A frequently encountered deciduous tree here is Red Alder. Its bark is sometimes as white as that of the eastern birch.

The giant leaves of skunk cabbage can be recognized in damp spots along the trail. Named for the pungent odor that they release in the spring, these marsh plants have large

succulent yellow flowers in early summer and their distinctive leaves are prominent later in the summer. The path remains in the cool, dark forest for most of its length.

Only 3 miles into the Park on the Carbon River road is the trailhead for a pleasant forest hike to a pretty lake, aptly named Green Lake. The distance is short, only 2.0 miles to the lake, and the trail is excellent. It gains a little over 1000 feet, but does so gradually by means of short switchbacks as it follows the course of Ranger Creek. The start of the hike is in deep forest.

Part way up, the trail tunnels under a large tree that fell across it, probably during a storm. As the trail begins to level off, there is a glimpse of the lake through the trees. Notice the vivid color of the water. Green Lake gets its name and its color by reflecting the color of the trees that surround it, especially the timbered slopes that hug it at the right. The southern horizon is occupied by peaks that make up part of Rust Ridge, northwest of Mowich Lake. The shore of the lake near its outlet is a pleasant place for a leisurely lunch before heading back to the Carbon River.

Hike 89 – Chenuis Falls

map pg. 224

A short but rewarding trip from the Carbon River road is the trail to Chenuis Falls, just across the river from the road. The trailhead is marked by a sign at a small parking area along the left hand side of the road. Highlights of the trip include the log bridges crossing the wild Carbon River. These normally have to be built and installed new each summer, as the river washes them away in the winter or spring.

It's only a short trip past the bridges up a slope to Chenuis Falls. The trail has a short spur that provides a fine view of the complex of these handsome falls of Chenuis Creek.

For completeness, this brief description is included of an abandoned trail that presently leads nowhere and does it awkwardly. The trail shows up on old maps as continuing upslope from the Carbon River to the Park boundary and beyond, but it is not maintained by the Park Service and is open and usable for only a mile or so before downed logs and thick brush make it unfriendly for going farther.

To try out this trail, proceed as described for Hike 89 to Chenuis Falls and find the continuing trail to the right past the falls. It ascends by switchbacks up the western ridge of Tirzah Peak, the northernmost peak of the Chenuis Mountain Range.

The trail soon fades as it climbs. This adventurer gave up after encountering too many logs barring the way, some two miles above the river, so the mysteries of the upper trail and the reason for its existence remain. Possibly it is a remnant of a north boundary trail.

A pleasant and easy loop trip from the end of the Carbon River road is the 6 mile round trip from the Ipsut Creek Campground along the upper Carbon River. This trail trip has at least three highlights: the views of the river on the way up, the swinging bridge across the river at the top of the loop, and the unusual forest passed through on the way back. It's nearly level the whole way so there is plenty of time to savor these features.

The first 1.6 miles are on the Wonderland Trail, parts of which follow an old road long ago converted to trail. Floods from the temperamental Carbon River have damaged the trail frequently and the Park Service often has had to reroute sections. Initially the trail is in forest, though there are occasional talus slope openings where it passes through thickets of salmonberries and vine maples. The river usually divides in two near here and the trail follows along its western channel.

A trail intersection is encountered at 1.6 miles. The left-hand branch is signed as the Northern Loop Trail, heading towards Windy Gap (Hike 94). This is where the loop part of the trip begins. This description takes the right-hand branch, which is the Wonderland Trail. It provides a counterclockwise direction around the loop; of course, one can do it in the reverse direction as well.

As the trail swings around to the right it leaves the forest and travels close to the river bed. Views of Rainier and glimpses of the dark mound that is the Carbon Glacier become available. About 0.8 miles from the Windy Gap junction the trail crosses Cataract Creek on a small bridge beneath a cataract.

Above and north of the bridge is the Carbon River Camp, located among storm-downed logs. Also here is the junction with the trail to Seattle Park (Hike 99), which continues on to Mowich Lake (Chapter 10).

A couple of tenths of a mile farther brings the hiker to a marvelous solution to the rampaging nature of the Carbon River. The Park Service has placed one of its swinging suspension bridges here to carry us across the river. This bridge can be lowered and pulled clear of the river in the winter and redeployed in the late spring, after danger of violent flooding is past. For many hikers the passage across the bridge, which sways with each step, is a special thrill.

The view from the center of the bridge upstream is of the snout of the glacier, its grayish debris-covered bulk looking more like a stream of rock than a stream of ice.

On the far side of the bridge the trail divides. To the right is the continuation of the Wonderland Trail, which heads up along the east side of the glacier and on to glorious

Moraine Park (Hike 93). To the left is the rest of the loop trip, heading down along the east side of the river. Here the trail passes through an unusual and particularly friendly section of forest. The ground is rocky and the rocks are softened by a covering of moss and ferns. The trees are modest in size and demeanor.

There are other forests like this in the Park and their origins are clear. Wherever a river (or glacier) formerly flowed before changing paths many years ago, the rocky bed eventually was seeded by flowers and shrubs and trees. In cases where the river has not returned to these channels for several decades, the vegetation has had a chance to settle in and become a forest. All the trees in such a forest have the same maximum age, set by the date of the departure of water and ice. This fact gives the woods a distinct character different from that of the ancient forests nearby, where trees range in age up to hundreds of years.

The trail passes through these lonely and enchanted woods for a little over a mile before coming to an intersection. Off to the right is the Northern Loop Trail, an alternate route for Wonderlanders (Hike 125). It ascends steeply to Windy Gap (Hike 94) and on to Sunrise. For the Carbon River Loop trip, take the trail to the left, which returns to the road at the Ipsut Creek Campground in about 1.8 miles. Of course, the route has to recross the river, which it does on temporary log bridges.

Hikers from the road at Ipsut Creek have a relatively easy opportunity to visit one of Rainier's most unusual glaciers. Following the Wonderland Trail from the campground, it is only 3.5 miles to strikingly close-up encounters with the Carbon Glacier.

This remarkable sheet of ice has many outstanding properties, but the most obvious is the fact that its lower parts have carved a path through veins of coal-bearing rock, giving it its name and its unique black color. The rocky debris from the sides of its steep lower channel cover the ice with blackish rock and dust with the weird result that you see black ice, but, unlike that encountered on winter city streets, this black ice is tens or hundreds of feet thick.

In fact the thickness of the glacier is another of its unusual properties. It has a large area, some 3 square miles, making it Rainier's third largest glacier, but it has the mountain's greatest maximum thickness (700 feet), the greatest volume (25 billion cubic feet) and greatest length (5.7 miles). And of all the glaciers in the lower 48 states, its terminus reaches to the lowest altitude at 3500 feet.

The first part of the route is described for Hike 91, which will bring you to the famous swinging bridge. Turn right beyond the bridge to follow the Wonderland Trail up to the glacier. The high mound of the terminus rises above the river as you look south.

The distance to where the ice is close at hand is only about a half mile. The trail follows the glacier's east side for almost 3 miles, but this trip need only bring you to the ice cliffs of the lower glacier for you to witness its remarkable character.

It's important to stay on the trail here. Though the ice may look solid and inviting, there are frequent avalanches of rock on the glacier surface that make its margins quite unreliable and dangerous.

A good turn-around point is Dick Creek, crossed by the Wonderland Trail on a log bridge.

After a good look at this unique geological feature, the return trip is a comfortable 3.5 miles back. To vary the route, one can take the eastside trail instead of crossing the river on the swinging bridge.

The trail to Moraine Park is one of the most varied and scenic trails in the Park's north side. It includes travel in deep forest, a thrilling trip on a suspension bridge, a close-up encounter with a glacier and a crossing of a glorious alpine meadow under the most spectacular of Mt. Rainier's cliffs.

The trip is fairly long for a day trip, totaling 6.5 miles one-way from the end of the Carbon River Road. It follows the Wonderland Trail all of the way, except for the short access trail from the parking area to the WT. The early parts of the trail are described in the sections for Hikes 91 and 92, which cover the parts from the trailhead to the Dick Creek Camp, along the Carbon Glacier. The trail stays close to the glacier for about a quarter mile, providing excellent views of the blackish ice and its rough and tumble rock-covered surface.

Across the glacier to the west are glimpses of the meadow-covered slopes of Seattle Park (Hike 99).

The trail leaves the glacier upon encountering Moraine Creek, which occupies a narrow valley separated from the glacier by a thin ridge. The trail is moderately steep as it ascends this forested valley towards the high country. Breaks in the trees provide promises of the meadowlands to come.

The left of the trail is nearly overhung by the cliffs of Old Desolate, a thousand feet above.

The trail levels as it enters the flat part of Moraine Park, where the grassy meadows begin.

Another turn brings the hiker to the special view of Mt. Rainier for which this meadow is famous. The northern face of the mountain consists of an immense cliff called Willis Wall, named for an early geologist who explored this part of the mountain in the 1890's. It is more than a mile wide and its nearly vertical face is 3000 feet from the snow and ice slopes at the top to the Carbon Glacier at the bottom. Mountain climbers have found routes up the Wall to the summit, but the way is extremely dangerous, as avalanches continually and unpredictably tumble from top to bottom. It's an unusual hour in summer when the rumble of an avalanche is not heard from the trail in Moraine Park.

The parkland is extensive, brilliant with flowers in summer and red with autumn colors in fall.

The Wonderland Trail continues on, of course. It gradually leaves the flat meadows and ascends the ridge towards the east, bound for Mystic Lake.

Ambitious hikers with a yen for the high and lonely should consider the trail to Windy Gap. The trip is steep and long, 3400 feet in elevation gain and 6 miles in length one way, but the payoff at the top is worth it. Windy it sometimes is, but on a sunny day the Gap is a paradise of high meadows, hidden tarns and expansive views.

The trail is part of the Northern Loop Trail (Hike 78). It begins at the end of the Carbon River Road at the Ipsut Creek campground and starts out up the river on the Wonderland Trail. A mile and a half from the trailhead is the Northern Loop junction. The way to Windy Gap is the left-hand trail, marked by a small trail sign pointing east down through the woods towards the river.

This trail emerges onto the wide, rocky, river bed to find a different scene every year. The Carbon River is a wild one, continually changing its path in its torrential trip to the lowlands, sometimes wiping out trails, bridges and roads in its way. The trail crews usually find the log bridge here completely gone each spring and they have to make a new bridge every year.

 Often the river is braided here so that it takes more than one bridge to get entirely across it. On the east side of the bridge (or bridges) the trail divides again. The trail to the right heads upstream to rejoin the Wonderland Trail at the Swinging Bridge and the left-hand choice is the Northern Loop Trail, going straight up to Windy Gap.

Actually, "straight" is not quite the right word. The trail switchbacks its way up. There are some 25 switchbacks from the river to the pass. About 2/3rds of the way up the trail leaves most of the forest behind. Above to the left are the colorful Yellowstone Cliffs that make up the south face of Tyee Peak.

A sign indicates arrival at the Yellowstone Cliffs backcountry camp, which is nicely placed in a grove of trees with a view of its namesake cliffs. Beyond the camp are more switchbacks as the trail continues to gain altitude.

Now the views begin. The trail is in a wide basin with Tyee Peak, part of the Chenuis Mountain Range, to the north and Crescent Mountain to the south. Across the valley to the west are massive Mother Mountain and Gove and Arthur Peaks

As the trail nears the summit it winds its way through groves of miniature trees, mostly Mountain Hemlock and Subalpine Firs. The trail becomes paved with flagstones

The picturesque shelf of Windy Gap lies ahead where the south fork of tiny Spukwush Creek flows down the rocky slopes.

At the top at last, Windy Gap is found to be a beautiful saddle of meadows and lakes. Two small lakes lie to the left of the trail, reached by a sketchy side trail through the meadows. The largest lake is close to the trail on the right. Rising above the Gap to the east is the sharp spire of Sluiskin Mountain, 7026 feet high.

There's a side trip from Windy Gap that reaches a unique geological feature, a volcanic natural bridge. Unlike the famous bridges of Utah, which are formed by stream erosion in sedimentary rocks, this one was formed by the erosion of softer volcanic deposits under a hard layer of andesite lava. The narrow bridge has a span of some 150 feet and is nearly 200 feet high.

The distance from Windy Gap is about a mile on a spur trail from the Northern Loop Trail. We have no photographs of it, but there are excellent published black and white photos in the books by Filley and by Spring and Manning, listed in the Introduction.

To complete the page we reproduce below a photograph of Hickson Natural Bridge, which will be published in our forthcoming book on hiking in southern Utah.

Lake James is reached with about equal difficulty from either the Carbon River or from Sunrise. Its distance from either makes a round trip a very long day's journey or a reasonably easy overnighter. The distance to the lake on the Northern Loop Trail is 8.2 miles from the Carbon River road and 12 miles from the Sunrise parking lot. There is a backcountry camp near the lake that would make a reasonable place for backpackers to stay if it's open (reservations are required). Otherwise, there are camps at Yellowstone Cliffs and at Fire Creek.

To reach the lake from Carbon River, leave the parking lot on the spur to the Wonderland Trail and follow it south to the signed intersection about 1.6 miles from the trailhead. Cross the river on the log bridges and come to another trail junction. Follow the arrows to Windy Gap (Hike 94) and Lake James.

At Windy Gap the trail tops the pass and turns abruptly downward into the forest.

A photograph of the lake from a distance is given in the section on the Northern Loop (Hike 78).

The trail from the Carbon River road to Ipsut Pass makes a strenuous day trip, more noted for the good exercise it provides than for the scenery. The distance is nearly 4 miles and the elevation gain is 2800 feet. However there are rewards, as the views from the top of the trail towards the east are excellent (and it's only 1.5 miles more from there to scenic Mowich Lake).

The trip starts at the Ipsut Creek Campground trailhead, which leads to the Wonderland Trail, where signs direct hikers either to the Carbon Glacier or to Ipsut Pass. Turning right, the route begins its ascent of the steep slopes, roughly following Ipsut Creek. The first half mile is gradual and then, after a switchback, the trail becomes more vertical. Looking up towards the Pass, its steep and brushy nature is evident.

The last few tenths of a mile are the steepest, involving several switchbacks. When the top is finally reached, be sure to rest a while, looking out to the east and down to the depths of the Ipsut Valley and distant Carbon River.

A fairly interesting trip, mostly in forest but with views of river and creek, can be made from Ipsut Creek Campground to Cataract Valley Camp. The one-way distance is 4.3 miles. Follow the route of the Wonderland Trail towards the Carbon Glacier, leaving it at the bridge over Cataract Creek.

Turn right past the bridge on the trail signed for Spray Park and Mowich Lake and begin an easy ascent along the valley of Cataract Creek. The cliffs of Mother Mountain rise above the trail to the right. Soon the trail enters a desolate area, where an extremely violent windstorm occurred in 1984. On each side of trail is the evidence of destruction, with giant logs piled helter-skelter on the forest floor. Young trees are promising that the forest will rise again, but it will take a hundred years to erase the damage of this one big blow.

Cataract Valley Camp is just to the right of the trail about 1.3 miles from the Wonderland Trail junction. It is a relatively large camp, with 7 individual sites and a group site. It's set nicely in a level, sunny group of trees and two streams pass conveniently through the camp area.

Seattle Park is a complex of meadows and rocks, lying above timberline to the west of the Carbon Glacier. It can be reached by trail, but the trail only samples a fraction of its many beauties. This description provides a guide to the parkland, including areas that must be reached cross country. People without navigational skills and experience should not leave the trail, as the maze of ridges and valleys that make up the park can be confusing and dangerously so.

First we describe the way to the fringes of Seattle Park that can be reached by trail. Take the Wonderland Trail to Cataract Creek and then the trail to the west and up Cataract Valley, as described for Hike 98. Above Cataract Valley Camp the trail turns south and switchbacks up the valley of Marmot Creek. There's nearly a thousand feet of elevation gain in the woods along this creek. The valley narrows and soon the trail is following close to the creek as both approach timberline.

The trail emerges from the trees and ascends through the glorious meadows of the upper Marmot Creek Valley. This is the start of the traverse along the north edge of Seattle Park.

All this is under the rugged cliffs of Mother Mountain to the north.

As an accompaniment to the trail, Marmot Creek provides both audio and visual delights. At one point the creek slides noisily down a rock slide in its bed.

An important place is reached where the creek tumbles down a slope and passes under a trail bridge. This is where the best side trip to the rest of Seattle Park begins.

Scrambling about in a National Park is usually a very bad idea. There are at least two reasons for this. First, the wilderness can be confusing and dangerous. Every year people become disoriented and lost, requiring expensive rescues; public entities now can charge you the full costs of your rescue. If you leave the trail, be really sure that you have all of the "ten essentials" (see Chapter 1 for the list) and that you have been trained in wilderness navigation.

The second reason is for the sake of the National Parks. Every step you take off of a trail potentially destroys some part of the Park. If you step on a plant, even a tiny little alpine plant, it may die and another may not replace it for years. If others follow your track a permanent new scar on the landscape will be made. If others don't follow your track, a network of scars can build up. In the more than 50 years that we have hiked at Mt. Rainier, we have noticed great harm resulting from off-trail travel in the high country, especially in popular areas. The Park Service is doing what it can, but it needs all of us to help. Therefore, if you follow the rest of this description of Seattle Park, remember not to go there until you're an experienced wilderness traveler and not to step anywhere except on rocks where your boot prints can't harm the fragile meadows.

With that in mind, here are some views of a scramble up into Seattle Park. First follow the creek bed up its tiny valley to a bouldery plateau.

A little higher on the plateau is a rock shelf with a charming double waterfall.

Some of the large rock formations look almost like Henry Moore sculptures (or is it the other way around?

An alpine park must, of course, have a pond.

But what about Mt. Rainier? Can't it be seen from this high, scenic park? Yes, from a bit farther south, where the great white mountain looms above the cliffs that form the southern edge of Seattle Park.

Chapter 10 – The Mowich Lake Region

Mowich Lake, the Park's largest, can be reached on a gravel road that enters the Park from the west. The road leaves the Carbon River Road to the right before it reaches the Park, and gains about 3500 feet before ending at the lake. The Mowich Lake Road roughly follows an old horse path that was a common route to the mountain in the late 1800's.

Mowich Lake is the center for several excellent trail trips. The Wonderland Trail passes through and there are several popular trips that begin here, such as those to Eunice Lake (Hike 103) and Spray Park (Hike 106).

The lake itself, of course, is also an attraction. There is a short trail that goes along the south side of the lake, providing some nice views, both of the lake and the surrounding mountains. At the road end are a crude picnic area and campground. Most campsites are right on the surface of the gravel road.

A short trail along the east side of the lake leads to a handsome, traditional ranger's cabin. Most of the old cabins are no longer occupied throughout the season, but are kept ready for occasional use when needed.

Mt. Rainier is not visible from the campground, but nice views of it can be had by following the Wonderland Trail towards the north, along the west side of the lake.

Hike 100 – The Paul Peak Trail map pg. .224

The Paul Peak Trail is a popular early and late season trail, as it is open when higher destinations in the region are still under snow. Its high point is on the southern slope of Paul Peak at 4200 feet. The trail is almost entirely in forest with very few views, but the forest has variety and is well worth the visit.

The trailhead is on the Mowich Lake Road at a parking area (with restrooms) about a mile inside the Park. The trail itself is just over 3 miles long, but it's common to continue on down the valley another half mile on the Wonderland Trail to visit the North Mowich River.

The trail begins downward with a fairly steep section, followed by a switchback and a gentler descent into the valley of Meadow Creek. The forest is mainly made up of the "Big Three" of the lower forests: Douglas Fir, Western Hemlock and Western Red Cedar.

Splashes of sunlight pierce the dense ceiling of evergreen branches. Part way down there's a small clearing, a rocky talus slope bordered by vine maples, colorful in the autumn.

A half mile from the trailhead, Meadow Creek is reached and crossed on a planked bridge. Beyond the creek the trail ascends gently along the west side of Paul Peak. Several different kinds of ferns (especially bracken, maidenhair and deer ferns) occupy the undergrowth and mushrooms abound in season.

As the trail turns towards the east, the forest changes. It becomes lighter and drier and the undergrowth is sparser.

258

Without its being obvious, the trail reaches its high point not far beneath the summit of modest Paul Peak. Off to the left the forest is open, letting in sunlight on a clear day. Soon glimpses of Mt. Rainier are possible (what a realtor would call "peek-a-boo views"), barely, through the trees. Also bits of the valley below can be seen. Then suddenly the trail turns downward and descends with many switchbacks to its end at a junction with the Wonderland Trail. One can turn around here, or, if wanting further exploration, one can turn left and follow the Wonderland up to Mowich Lake to make a strenuous loop trip (Hike 101) or turn right to head down to the North Mowich River and beyond (Hike 107).

A fairly long forest trip can be patched together by combining the Paul Peak Trail (Hike 100) and the Grindstone Trail (Hike 102) with a section of the Wonderland Trail (Hike 125) to make a loop trip. It isn't perfect, as there are a little over two miles of road involved (of course, if two cars are available this problem can be avoided). The total mileage on the trails is about 8.5, depending on how much of the Grindstone Trail is used.

The loop can be taken in either direction. We'll follow a clockwise route here, but one can think of advantages to going either way. Starting at the Mowich Lake campground, the trail descends to the south. For the first half mile, down a few steep switchbacks, the route is shared with the popular Spray Park Trail (Hike 106), so other hikers will probably be passed. There's a nice, slightly broken (in 2003) log bridge crossing a small unnamed stream.

At a trail junction the Spray Park trail takes off to the left, while you and the Wonderland Trail continue on down to the right. The trail descends fairly steeply, heading towards Crater Creek. This creek was named a hundred years ago when Mowich Lake, its source, was called Crater Lake. The name of the lake was changed when geologists pointed out that, in spite of its roughly circular shape, the lake is not in a volcanic crater, but a depression formed by glacial action. The name of the lake was changed, but the authorities forgot to change the name of its stream.

Where the trail crosses it, Crater Creek is divided into two streams by a rib of rocks. Simple log bridges are sufficient to get over each branch.

Just upstream from the bridges is a nice waterfall. It has no official name, but it could be called Crater Falls, in light-hearted defiance of the geologists. The trail continues down into Crater Creek Valley through deep forest until it reaches the Paul Peak Trail junction. Turning right, loop hikers will then begin an ascent through several switchbacks.

Upon reaching the top of this trail at the road, one either trudges up the road to the right or picks up the car left here earlier. If walking the road, the next trail will be the Grindstone Trail, described in Hike 102. It provides a pleasant shortcut to Mowich Lake, which it almost reaches, leaving only a short additional road walk near the top of the route.

Motorists on the Mowich Lake Road are sometimes curious about the two small trail signs that they pass near the top of the road. Labeled as the Grindstone Trail, they don't appear on most maps and few cars stop to explore them.

They're actually three short sections of an historical trail of over a hundred years ago. In the 1890's there was a horse trail to what was then called Crater Lake, proceeding up the Carbon River Valley from the mining town of Wilkenson and then up the ridge to the lake. Later, when the "Round the Mountain Highway" was being planned, the route of this old trail was adopted by the road builders, who had decided that the Ipsut Pass was too steep for a more direct route from the Carbon Glacier region. After the circum-mountain road idea was abandoned, the present road was built, opened to the public in 1955. The upper part of the road involves some wide switchbacks, while the old trail went up more directly. The Grindstone Trail is the remnant of that old trail where it intersects the windings of the upper road. Its name comes from a trail-builders' camp that was located somewhat lower and that was originally called "Bark Town" (the cabins were made of bark), later changed to "Grindstone Camp."

Although there are three walkable sections of this old trail, only the upper two are presently (2003) being maintained. We'll describe all three, though the lower one is

somewhat hard to find. There's no sign for it, so one must drive slowly, keeping a watch out for the faint beginnings of the trail. To find the bottom of the lower trail, drive 2.0 miles up from the Paul Peak Trailhead. Watch for two very small waterfalls on the left side of the road. Between them is a steep, bare path; this is the trail. If you find yourself beginning the sharp turn of a switchback, you've gone too far; go back down and try again.

Once up the short beginning slope the trail turns to the right and passes among some excellent huckleberry bushes. After crossing a doubtful bridge, it then turns upslope and passes a small marshy meadow. Next are two more ancient-looking bridges and, after hopping over some downed trees, the hiker will arrive at the road again. About 20 yards down the road on the left is the continuation of the Grindstone Trail, in this case marked by a trail sign.

The middle section of the trail is nicely maintained (though there is a sign about 1/4th mile up that warns of the lack of maintenance). A nearly new bridge crosses a seasonal stream. The forest is attractive, mostly made up of Western Hemlocks, a few Douglas Firs and some Noble Firs with their remarkable cones pointing straight up. The middle section ends again at the road. A trail sign is across the road and it points the way to the upper section. The forest in the upper section is a little different. There are a few more high altitude tree types and more sunny, open areas.

The trail ends where it emerges from the woods into a small meadow area close to the top of the road.

From here there are sketchy hints of a continuation of the trail, but it's only a small distance to the lake by road, so there's not a lot of reason to try to find the remains of the Grindstone Trail's last few hundred yards.

Hike 103 – Eunice Lake

map pg. .224

A short and rewarding trail trip from Mowich Lake is the one to Eunice Lake. Only about 2½ miles one way, this trip reaches a spectacular alpine lake, nestled below the steep rocky slopes of Tolmie Peak. At an elevation of 5100 feet, Eunice Lake is in the zone of subalpine meadows, with fields of flowers in season and low bush blueberries to both color and flavor the autumn.

Hikers usually begin the trip from the parking area at Mowich Lake, a few hundred yards west of the end of the road. A nicer start can be made from near the ranger station, just north of the road end and campground, as that portion of the trail skirts the lakeshore in a marshy meadow. Either way connects to the Wonderland Trail, which is followed for about 1.5 miles to Ipsut Pass (see Hike 97 for a description of the Pass). Along much of the way the trail follows the shore of Mowich Lake.

At Ipsut Pass, the trail to Eunice Lake leaves the Wonderland Trail, turning off to the left. It stays in forest for a mile or so, losing a little altitude, but basically staying about level. Then after a couple of short switchbacks the trail breaks out into open meadows. Nearing Eunice Lake, which is just visible in the distance, it first passes a small pond.

Eunice Lake itself is a fairly large lake, covering about 15 acres. Its shores are rocky and scenic, with many bays and inlets along the south shoreline.

The placid lake waters reflect the steep cliffs of Tolmie Peak. The lookout building is conspicuous at the crest of the peak (Hike 104).

The trail circles around to the left, reaching the shallow west shore, where the Tolmie Peak trail starts up.

There are several small ponds to the west of the lake. Unfortunately, the meadows around the lake have invited hikers to wander beyond the official trail. This has led to a random network of paths, scarring the otherwise sublime views. Most current hikers are aware of the fragile nature of these high meadows and stay on the Park's trails, but a few have forgotten themselves and have left boot prints and dying meadow plants where they shouldn't be.

A look back at the meadowy hills with a pond in the foreground provides a nice view of the mountain that rises above to the south.

Hikers to Eunice Lake will notice that the trail continues on beyond the lake. If the weather's good, this continuation can lead to marvelous views from a mountain top. Tolmie Peak Lookout is one of the circle of lookouts around the mountain, established in the 1930's for fire detection. Others are Shriner Peak, Mt. Fremont and Gobbler's Knob, all with excellent trails to them. No longer needed for fire lookouts, the buildings are now maintained as historical buildings and to provide information for hikers, as they are often occupied in the summers by volunteers.

The trail to the lookout from Eunice Lake is only about ½ mile, though it's fairly steep, gaining 570 feet from the lakeshore. The distance from the parking lot at Mowich Lake is 3.2 miles. The very pleasant portion of the trail to Eunice Lake is described in Hike 103. Hikers to the lookout should continue west along the shore of the lake (staying on the obvious main trail and forswearing the temptation to patronize the meadow-killing side trails). The lookout building will be visible above the cliffs beyond the lake.

Upon leaving the meadows, the trail up begins to enter a scattered forest of subalpine trees. Broad switchbacks help to gain altitude on the steep slope. The large white globes of bear grass line the way in summer.

During the entire climb of the slope it is difficult to keep going without stops to gaze at the view. The last bit of trail passes through a small forest of dwarfish subalpine firs.

Finally the lookout is reached. On a clear summer day there are likely to be several others enjoying the view, which is best from the deck that wraps around the upper story.

Turn clockwise to view the entire horizon. The view to the east is of Tolmie Peak's east ridge, with Chenuis Mountain in the distance. There is often a snow field close-by to the northeast even in August. In the distance above it is the valley of Ranger Creek, leading down to the Carbon River beyond the ridge to the left.

Off to the north, beyond the clearcuts in the National Forest on the other side of the Carbon River, the snowy summits of Glacier Peak and Mt. Baker are on the horizon.

The view southwest from the lookout

includes a pond in the meadows west of Eunice Lake and the truncated cone of Mt. St. Helens in the distance.

The view southeast is of Castle Peak and Mother Mountain, with the craggy tops of the peaks of the Northern Loop trail in the farther distance.

Straight down to the south is a great view of Eunice Lakeand its network of official and illicit trails. The Mowich Lake road is visible beyond.

Of course, the dominating feature of the view from the lookout is the snowy centerpiece of this National Park.

Hike 105 – Spray Falls map pg. .224

The trip to Spray Falls is a short (2.1 miles) hike from Mowich Lake, easy to do in a half day. The trail begins at the road end, following the Wonderland Trail for ¼ mile downward to a trail junction. Take the left-hand trail, signed to Spray Park. The trail stays in the forest for most of its way to the falls, though there are occasional views, as this one towards the cliffs to the south.

As the trail nears the top of Eagle Cliff, there is a short spur trail to a viewing platform, providing an excellent view of the mountain from the cliff top
.

Another short spur trail to the right follows, leading to a sideways view of Spray Falls, one of the Park's largest. The view of the falls is partly curtailed by intervening slopes, but the spray is there, often felt even from the trail.

Hike 106 – Spray Park map pg. .224

Spray Park is a popular destination from Mowich Lake and is often full of hikers on a sunny summer weekend day. Even with crowds it's a worthwhile trip, as the meadows are fine, the views are excellent and the park is large enough that people are usually dispersed fairly thinly.

The distance is about 3 miles, depending on how far up into the park one goes. To reach the highest parts of the park near permanent snowfields at 6400 feet, the distance is close to 4 miles.

The trip begins at the Mowich Lake campground where the Wonderland Trail comes up from the Mowich River to the south. Head down on the Wonderland for a few hundred yards to where the Spray Park Trail branches off to the left. The trail is nearly level, dipping briefly to cross Lee Creek and then traversing along the top of Eagle Cliff before reaching a viewing platform a little way below the trail. Shortly afterward the trail passes a back country camp called Eagle's Roost. Another spur trail farther on leads to a view of Spray Falls (Hike 105). From here the trail begins a serious upward climb, switchbacking

up along the Grant Creek Valley until it reaches the beginnings of the high country. The views open up as the trees thin and the trail begins to level off a bit.

There's almost a mile of trail through the park, taking you gradually up past rolling meadowlands, small tarns and a few rocky outcrops. In early summer Spray Park is a paradise of flowers, with avalanche lilies in profusion. Later in the summer, lupine and Indian paintbrush take over.

It is tempting here to leave the trail and wander through the meadows. This is not a good idea, as boots can be remarkably destructive. There are a few well-established way trails where the meadow plants have already been killed and a careful use of these might be permitted, especially if you hop from boulder to boulder where possible. Some lead to small, attractive ponds.

One can follow the official trail even higher. Although snow often stays in the upper park on into August, by late summer it's usually possible to head towards higher country.

At the top of the trail great views can be enjoyed. Ptarmigan Ridge lines the western horizon.

The trail goes on from its high point at 6400 feet, heading east down through Seattle Park (Hike 99) and the Carbon River.

The up and down trip to Sunset Park from Mowich Lake is a good overnighter, though very strong hikers might decide to do it in one day. The one-way distance is 10 miles and there is plenty of elevation gain and loss. The entire trip is on the Wonderland Trail, Hike 125. The trailhead is at the end of the Mowich Lake road at the western end of the campground. The trail starts steeply down through increasingly dense forest, following the valley of Crater Creek, the outlet of Mowich Lake.

In 3.7 miles the trail reaches its low point at the Mowich River shelters. After crossing the two branches of the river, the trail heads up again, with many switchbacks to help gain the 2000 feet in elevation difference. At the top of a ridge, part of The Colonnade, the trail levels off and passes through open country with some high-country forest, finally reaching the lakes of Sunset Park. There is a backcountry camp here, set among the 15 or so Golden Lakes. The lakes make up the headwaters of Rushingwater Creek, which flows west out of the Park

An ancient-looking patrol cabin is also here, though it is infrequently occupied. Be sure to stay on the trail. There are hundreds of acres of parkland in Sunset Park, all fragile and easily despoiled by random tramping.

Sunset Park gets its name from the fact that at sunset the view of the mountain can be quite beautiful. A soft pink light called the "alpenglow" illuminates the snow fields and glaciers for a few minutes as the sun sets in the west.

Also named for this sunset phenomenon is the high basin at the top of the Puyallup Glacier below Liberty Cap. The Sunset Amphitheater is a conspicuous ice bowl as seen from Sunset Park, as well as from other vantage points on the west side, such as from Gobbler's Knob (Hike 109).

The extent of Sunset Park can be appreciated in this distant view through the trees from Klapatche Ridge to the south.

Following the Wonderland Trail beyond Sunset Park a short distance brings one to a ghost forest of burned trees, from a long-ago forest fire

Chapter 11 – The Westside Road Region

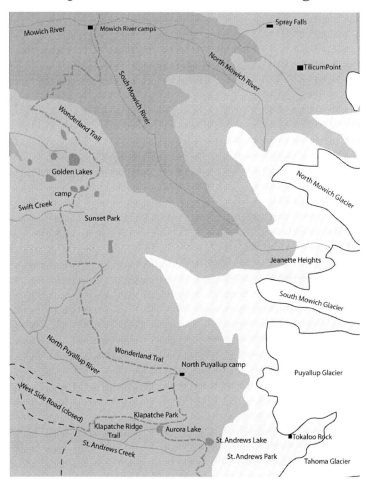

Map 14 Westside Road Region North (continued south on Map 2)

The Westside Road is a gravel road that for many years provided convenient access to most of Rainier's hikes to the parklands on the west. It extended from a junction just a mile inside the Nisqually Entrance to the north as far as the North Puyallup River. The road, completed in the 1930's, was conceived as part of a "round the mountain highway", which eventually was abandoned, first because of engineering problems and later because of the interruption of World War II. The idea of a highway encircling the mountain has in the mean time become unattractive. The millions of visitors each year are best concentrated in the areas that have appropriate facilities for auto-oriented visits, leaving a few areas in the park for wilderness trails.

Several catastrophic floods (the worst being in 1967 and 1987) washed out parts of the existing Westside Road. The floods were sudden and violent, one of them coming down through the (former) Tahoma Creek Campground with such force as to wash away many of the tables, and to deposit giant logs among the camp spots. The Park Service closed the road after each flood and it has remained closed at the 3 mile point since 1993.

The views from the road barrier give a hint about the nature of the problem. The valley to one side of the road has the broad, flat shape of a large river, which it temporaril y can be, and the trees in the flats are a mix of old, damaged or dead victims and small, young hopefuls.

The rest of the road may reopen some day, but the floods continue their destructive activity almost annually. Not wanting to repeat past experiences, including a 1988 flood that stranded 39 cars full of tourists, the Park Service has considered never reopening it, instead putting in a hikers' bus service from the present road barrier to Round Pass.

Hike 108 – Lake George

map pg. .278

The Lake George trailhead is 3.5 miles from the barrier on the Westside Road, so that much of the trip has to be negotiated by road-walking, bicycling or taking a hikers' bus if one is available. The trailhead is a few hundred feet south of Round Pass. From the road the hike to the lake is a pleasant mile through a quiet forest. At 4300 feet, Lake George is an intermediate-level lake, surrounded by Western Hemlocks and Douglas Firs. There is a backcountry camp, with a shelter and a ranger cabin nearby. A trail follows a beach along the west shoreline.

Viewed from the top of nearby Gobbler's Knob (Hike 109), the beach area along the east shore looks sunny and inviting.

Each of the fire lookout sites in the Park has a spectacular view of Rainier and its surroundings and Gobbler's Knob is a particularly grand example. From its heights ones sees the entire westside region of meadows and valleys, with the rugged cliffs of the Sunset Amphitheater and the cascading ice of several glaciers around them.

The trail is shared with Lake George as far as that lake (Hike 108). It continues on from the lake another fairly steep mile to the rocky top at 5485 feet. About half way there the trail passes a pretty, small lake locally called Gobbler's Pond.

Attentive readers will have noticed an inconsistency in the name of this and some other places in the Park: sometimes the name has an apostrophe and sometime it doesn't. The problem arises from the fact that mapmakers do not like names that include punctuation marks, which can be confused with geographic features on the maps. Thus Gobblers Knob does not have an apostrophe on maps, though it is a knob occupied (at least supposedly at one time) by something or someone that gobbled. The same issue arises for Indian Henry's Hunting Ground, which was named because a real person, nicknamed Indian Henry, hunted there, but maps designate it without an apostrophe. Note also that maps don't use periods for abbreviations, such as Mt. or Mtn. Mapmakers sometimes avoid the problem by spelling it out; for example they usually spell out Mount Rainier. In other cases they simply leave out the period, as in Satulick Mtn and St Andrews Park.

The trail switchbacks on up above Gobbler's Pond, providing a bird's eye view of its meadowy shoreline. The top is close, just beyond a final set of short switchbacks.

The expansive view of Rainier from the top is wonderful.

Goat Lake is almost in the National Park, but not quite. It is easily reached from the trail to Lake George and Gobbler's Knob, so many visitors hike there from the Park. The trail to Goat Lake, which goes on to Beljica Meadows and logging roads beyond, leaves the Gobbler's Knob Trail at the third switchback above Gobbler's Pond. It continues south up and over the ridge before descending to Goat Lake. The total distance from the Westside Road is 4 miles. Some hikers reach the lake (and Gobbers Knob) from the west, approaching via Forest Service roads.

The lake is on the west side of the ridge that connects Gobbler's Knob with the much bigger Mt. Wow. From the top of the lookout site, it looks a lot like a smaller version of Lake George; the two lakes are at almost exactly the same elevation (4300 feet) and thus are located in the same forest zone.

There are meadows to the south and a faint trail along the tree-lined shores, reached by a short spur trail that leaves left from the main trail as it skirts to the north of the lake.

This short trail was built in order to provide a shortcut from Round Pass to the South Puyallup River Trail, thus avoiding a long circuitous switchback. When the road beyond was closed for a period at Round Pass, the shortcut was a boon for hikers to Emerald Ridge and St. Andrews Park. It is about a mile long. When or if the Westside Road is opened again to its end, this trail will become superfluous.

Round Pass itself is a worthy, if modest goal. It is a high point on the road, providing a nice view of the mountain. Also there's a monument there of historical interest. In December, 1946, a military transport plane crashed on the South Tahoma Glacier above, taking the lives of all 32 Marines aboard. The plane is still buried in the ice and the stone monument at Round Pass serves as a memorial.

Anyone who's crossed it will surely rate the Tahoma Creek Bridge as one of the highlights of the trails on Rainier's west side. It is a suspension bridge, made of swinging cables and wooden planks, providing a thrill of the sort usually reserved for mountain climbing or parachuting. In fact, some hikers find it so exciting that they make the effort to get to it as a primary goal of a hike, in spite of its relative inaccessibility. Other hikers consider it altogether too exciting and proceed across it with breath held and eyes closed. On our most recent visit we met a park ranger who had been sent to the bridge from Longmire to help a Wonderland Trail hiker who had stopped, refusing to cross until someone came to help. The bridge is 250 feet long and swings in mid-air 100 feet above Tahoma Creek. Steel towers at each end support the cables to which the planks of the bridge floor are attached.

Even if you enjoy such thrills, there's a problem. The bridge is not easy to get to. Formerly there was no such difficulty. When the road was open, one could drive to the Tahoma Creek Campground and hike the 2.2 miles on the Tahoma Creek Trail to the bridge. But Tahoma Creek had other ideas. Its violent flooding took out the road, the campground, and part of the trail, too. The trail was severely damaged and was closed for several years. Check with the Park to be sure it is not closed before heading that way. If so, there are two much longer trail trips to choose as alternate routes. One can hike the Wonderland Trail from Longmire via Indian Henry's Hunting Ground (Hike 7), a total distance of 8.6 miles, or, if one bikes or otherwise can get to the South Puyallup River Trail on the Westside Road, it's a scenic 5.2 miles via Emerald Ridge (Hike 115).

Hike 113 – Indian Henry's from Tahoma Creek map pg. .278

There are three ways to reach Indian Henry's Hunting Ground, one of the most beautiful alpine parks of Rainier. The 5.2 mile route up Kautz Creek (Hike 2) is the shortest. The way from Longmire via Rampart Ridge (Hike 7) is the longest at 6.9 miles. The trip via Tahoma Creek is the most awkward because of the closure of the Westside Road. If the direct trail from the road is open (check with the Park Service for its condition), then it's an interesting trip. The trailhead is about 4.7 miles from the turn-off onto the Westside Road. The trail proceeds along the northern bank of the creek all the way to its intersection with the Wonderland Trail, a little over 2 miles from the trailhead, winding through forest at its edge above the creek's rocky canyon.

This forest is a fine example of a lowland virgin forest. It grows on the steep slope

formed by the once giant Tahoma Glacier. During the last ice age the glacier occupied the entire valley, where it cut out a steep-sided U-shaped profile. Trail hikers will see the effects in the form of steep slopes and rocky cliffs. Along the way there are several waterfalls made by small streams flowing down the steep slope to Tahoma Creek.

While it's exciting to imagine the havoc that resulted when the creek burst in a sudden flood down this valley, today's excitement might turn out, depending on your level of acrophobia, to be the bridge that now crosses the creek (Hike 114). The trail from the Westside Road reaches the Wonderland Trail a short distance from the crossing, to the right. The tumultuous creek looks innocent enough in mid-summer.

286

At the far end of the bridge the trail begins an upward path, first along the edge of the creek's canyon and then through forest in several switchbacks. Towards the mountain the view is of the snout of the South Tahoma Glacier. This is a small glacier, separate from the main Tahoma Glacier to the north. Between the two glaciers is a knife-edge rock fin called the Tahoma Cleaver. Glacier Island separates them at lower elevations. The terminus of the South Tahoma is almost unrecognizable because of its cover of rocky debris.

Views out to the west through the trees are of the terminus of the main Tahoma Glacier and the steep face of Glacier Island (see Hike 115).

After three stream crossings, the trail begins to emerge into high ground, with sub-alpine trees and the first flowery meadows. This is the beginning of Indian Henry's Hunting Ground. A half mile of meandering through this parkland brings you past the Mirror Lakes turn-off (Hike 114) and to the junction with the Kautz Creek Trail (Hike 2). In summer the slopes and valleys are filled with blue lupine and sprinklings of other alpine flowers.

A side trail from the Wonderland Trail at Indian Henry's leads to a scene that has probably been distributed more widely than any other picture of Mt. Rainier ever. During his presidency, Franklin Roosevelt, an avid stamp collector, took a personal interest in

US postage stamps, encouraging a wider variety of stamp designs than was customary at that time. One of the results was a series of stamps with various American scenes displayed on them. On August 3, 1934, a stamp was issued that showed Mt. Rainier as reflected in one of the small Mirror Lakes of Indian Henry's. This popular stamp brought the mountain into the homes of millions of Americans.

There are four Mirror lakes, though three are quite small. Getting to them is easy, providing that you've already reached Indian Henry's Hunting Ground (Hikes 2, 7, and 114). The side trail is just under a mile in length, taking one through the heart of Indian Henry's and up to its upper meadows near the foot of Pyramid Peak. Copper and Iron Mountains are to the east.

And the mountain, of course, dominates the view, rising above the lakes, sometimes in the mist, hardly changed at all since its famous postal debut 70 years ago.

Icefalls, colorful moraines, green meadows and flower fields, - these are the rewards of hikers who make their way to Emerald Ridge. Formerly easy to reach from the Westside Road, access to the trail is now a little more awkward, with that road closed. However, by biking or hoofing or taking the promised hikers' bus, it's possible to reach the beginning of one of the west side's most glorious trail trips. The present trailhead is a little over a mile past Round Pass on the Westside Road. Formerly it was popular to reach Emerald Ridge via the Tahoma Creek Trail, which Tahoma Creek damaged by washing part of it away, so now the surest route may be from farther on via the South Puyallup River Trail. As the Ridge is on the Wonderland Trail, it's also possible to reach it from the south from Longmire by way of Indian Henry's (Hike 7) or from the north from Mowich Lake via Sunset Park and Klapatche Park (Hikes 107 and 116). These routes, of course, are only practical as overnighters.

The distance from the trailhead on the Westside Road to the top of Emerald Ridge is 3.9 miles. The first half is in very nice forest and the second half is along the edge of a cliff above the Tahoma Glacier, providing marvelous views. An "aerial view" from Gobbler's Knob shows how the wooded ridge extends up into the land of rock and ice. The upper trail follows the edge of the forest and meadows in this picture.

The South Puyallup River Trail ascends gently up the valley just south of its namesake river, joining the Wonderland Trail at 1.6 miles. Hikers to Emerald Ridge will turn right at the junction, which is at 4000 feet. Views open up soon, as the trail nears the rubble of the Tahoma Glacier's terminal moraine. When the lower regions of the glacier are reached, notice the unusual orange and reddish color of the rocks and gravel that blanket the ice. It's possible to trace these colors back to the cliffs higher up that produced the colorful debris, cliffs of rocks colored by past hydrothermal activity. As the trail leads up along the edge of the ridge, the views of ice expand. Watch for mountain goats below; on two occasions we watched goats there as they made their way carefully over the jumbled ice. Above the ice to the north are unnamed waterfalls, splashing down from snowfields on the lower parts of Puyallup Cleaver.

The name of the ridge becomes justified when the trail leaves the trees behind and enters the green meadows. Flowers, especially blue lupine, add color to the slopes.

Looking up from the trail, one sees the white snow-covered ice and can trace the place where the upper Tahoma Glacier flows out from near the summit of Mt. Rainier.

Above the trail to the left the glacier view expands. The highest point of the trail is at an elevation of 5600 feet. This is the prow of the ship-like ridge, with the Puyallup Glacier diverted off to the left and remnant ice and snowfields off to the right. In the 1930's and earlier there was ice flowing in both directions. The huge mound seen above you when you stand at the trail's summit is Glacier Island. Now it's more of a peninsula, but when it was named it was surrounded by ice. The Puyallup Glacier was at the left and the South Puyallup Glacier to the right, with the rocky island in between. Glacier Island's steep western side faces the trail.

The South Tahoma Glacier is now off to the right and in the foreground is the meltwater stream that flows where glacial ice once flowed a few decades ago.

Hikers with time to spare can continue on the Wonderland Trail down to the south to see the country that northbound hikers encounter on their way to the top of the ridge. The trail travels down through a valley made by the glacier's lateral moraine. Its smooth rocky surface is made up of gravel that was dumped by the glacial ice that was moving down (at the left) during the early part of the last century.

Gazing back up towards the ridge top, a hiker can contemplate the stagnant, rock-covered ice that has replaced the mighty glacier that once formed an ice-locked island.

A particularly stunning view of the mountain reflected in an alpine lake is a frequent feature of books and articles on Mt. Rainier National Park. The lake is Aurora Lake, the centerpiece of Klapatche Park. Formerly easy to get to, this marvelous region is now isolated by the closure of the Westside Road and is reachable only after a long road trip by boot, bike or bus or by a longer hike from Longmire or Mowich Lake. This relative isolation is undoubtedly a good thing for Klapatche Park, which had begun to look sadly overused in the decades before road closure.

To reach this area, one can get to the trailhead on the Westside Road about 11 miles from the road's beginning near the Nisqually Entrance. At mileage 3.0 the road is closed to private cars and farther travel is done by bicycle or by other means. The shortest trail up is the St. Andrews Creek Trail, which has a trailhead near Denman Falls. It is also possible to follow the road 3.5 miles farther and meet the Wonderland Trail at the North Puyallup bridge.

The St. Andrews Creek Trail follows its namesake creek through a pleasant forest. After about 1½ miles, the trail begins to switchback up towards the top of Klapatche Ridge to the left. Openings in the forest provide sunny interludes.

The trail proceeds along the top of the ridge where there are excellent views of the valley of the North Puyallup River and the upper regions of Sunset Park.

When the trail finally breaks out of the trees completely, the mountain is seen hovering over the green meadows of lower Klapatche Park. The climax view comes soon, when the trail reaches the main parkland and small, strategically-placed Aurora Lake with its famous reflection. The prominent tower in the left foreground is the bottom cliff of Puyallup Ridge.

There's a backcountry camp near the lake and plenty of flowers in the meadow to keep you here. But there's also an inviting trail visible above the lake to the south and it may be difficult to resist. It's the Wonderland Trail and it leads up to some worthwhile higher views in only a few tenths of a mile. The trail winds its way up along the south side of Aurora Peak. Along the way towards St. Andrews Park (Hike 117) it comes to openings to the east that providenice views of the mountain.

The extensive alpine parkland south of Klapatche Park is all part of St. Andrews Park. It includes a beautiful high alpine lake and flowery meadows, as well as rocky prominences and summer snowfields.

St. Andrews Park can be reached from either the south or the north. If Klapatche Park (Hike 116) is also part of your destination, then it's simplest to go there first and then to follow the Wonderland Trail a mile and a half south, up into the higher country of St. Andrews. Alternatively, it's possible to reach St. Andrews Park by taking the South Puyallup River Trail from the Westside Road and turning left at the junction with the Wonderland Trail near the bridge. It's 3.7 miles from the road to the high point in St. Andrews Park (this doesn't count the mileage that must be trekked on the road to get to the trailhead).

The extensive meadowlands of St. Andrews Park are visible in this telephoto view taken from Gobbler's Knob. Tokaloo Spire is prominent above the park.

This description will take the route from the road via the South Puyallup River Trail. It is a pleasant 1.6 miles from the road to the junction with the Wonderland Trail. Along the way are some excellent examples of basaltic columns, crystal-like formations made when basaltic lava solidified centuries ago.

The trail junction is near the South Puyallup Backcountry Camp. To reach St. Andrews Park, one takes a left turn on the Wonderland and crosses the South Puyallup River on a log bridge. Following a long series of switchbacks, the trail emerges in the meadows. Off to the west the clearcut forest outside the park contrasts with the ancient, unspoiled forest the trail has just passed through.

The high point of this trip, in two senses of the word, is St. Andrews Lake. It is at the highest elevation reached in the park (5800 feet) and it is an especially nice lake, set in a bowl of meadows with Mt. Rainier rising above it.

Chapter 12 – The Highway 410 Region

State Highway 410 is the road that takes Mt. Rainier visitors from Puget Sound east to the northern and eastern parts of the National Park. It begins east of Tacoma, passes through Sumner and Buckley and in Enumclaw begins its forest and mountain journey up away from the populated flatlands. Following the White River valley and never far from the river, the first forested miles are in tree farming country. Logging activity is always close by and recently-planted forests are designated by signs giving the years of harvest and replanting.

Before it enters the Mt. Baker-Snoqualmie National Forest, Highway 410 passes through a remarkable park that is well worth a stop and a hike. It is Federation Forest State Park, an oasis of virgin forest in the midst of the tree farmed hills (Hike 124).

Just beyond the State Park the highway reaches the town of Greenwater, the last source of food, gasoline and supplies. The Greenwater River joins the White River here and it lends its name to the area, especially to the east of the highway. A little over two miles beyond the town is a well-used road, Forest Service Road 70, which follows the Greenwater River through vast areas of logged off and soon to be logged off land.

The next intersection occurs just beyond a small rest area (one can rest there but there are no restrooms). There is a nice view of Mt. Rainier, a display shelter and parking for several cars. Just beyond it, Forest Road 73 leaves Highway 410 to the right (if you are southbound). A quarter of a mile along this road are two trailheads: on the east side of the bridge over the White River is a trail to the Dalles Campground and on the west side of the bridge is one end of FS Trail 1174 (Hike 123). Farther on, a little less than a mile from the bridge, is a road to the left that goes up to the Suntop Lookout area (Hike 118). Five miles beyond the bridge FS 73 comes to the lower trailhead of the Huckleberry Creek Trail (Hike 82).

The Dalles Campground is a pleasant deep forest campground with facilities for most kinds of camping. At the northern edge of the campground is a remarkable Douglas Fir. It is 9 ½ feet in diameter and about 700 years old. A short signed trail leads the way.

Another feature of this campground worth a stop is the John Muir Nature Trail that loops down to the river and back, with display signs about the natural history of the forest and the river bottom. The nature trail is at the southern end of the campground.

The Highway Department has constructed a pull-out about a mile and a half past the Dalles Campground where there is a good view of Skookum Falls, across the river and high above the valley. In early summer it's a grand sight, but by autumn there is likely to be only a thin thread of water.

Nearby is an inconspicuous trailhead on the hillside to the left. This leads up into the Camp Sheppard trails area (Hike 122) and is one of several access points for this well-maintained maze of trails constructed by the Boy Scouts at Camp Sheppard. A second access trail is passed a few hundred yards farther on. The signed road to the left 2½ miles from the Dalles Campground leads to the Boy Scout Camp and to a well-equipped trailhead with restrooms and ample parking for trail users. Two additional inconspicuous trailheads to the left are found in the next 1½ miles of SR 410 beyond the Camp Sheppard Road.

Forest Service Road 7160 turns to the right from SR 410 and immediately crosses the river on a high bridge. At the farther side of the bridge is a trailhead parking area, serving the riverside trails both north and south from here. The trail follows the river, often high above it.

Just before reaching the National Park boundary, there is the small "community" of Silver Springs. On the right is the Silver Springs Campground. A telephone and a visitor's information cabin (formerly a ranger cabin) nestle among the trees in an attractive open forest. The springs themselves are worth a brief visit. On the left are some summer homes.

A paved road to the left a few hundred feet before the Park boundary leads to the extensive Crystal Mountain development, busy in the winter with skiing and other winter sports and in the summer with conferences and summer activities. Some trails can be accessed from the resort area (Hike 121).

From the Park boundary Highway 410 continues south, past the turn-off for the White River and Sunrise areas and on up to Cayuse Pass, where there is an intersection with the road to Ohanapecosh. Highway 410 reaches its high point at Chinook Pass, where it leaves the Park on its way to eastern Washington.

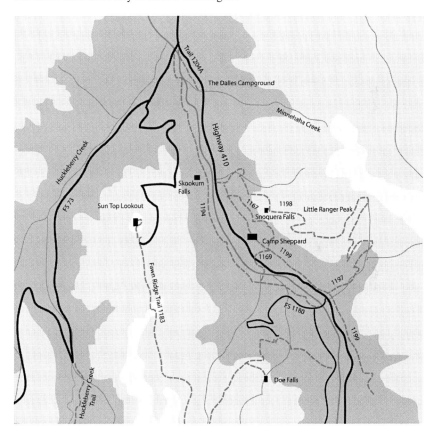

Map 15 The Highway 410 Region

A short and scenic hike to a spectacular lookout site with views in all directions, including a classic full view of Mt. Rainier: what could be better? Not much, unless the road to the top is open, in which case the summit of this scenic knob might be crowded with the car-borne multitudes. On our recent visits the road was closed and the hike was pure pleasure.

Suntop Mountain (sometimes spelled Sun Top) is reached by way of FS Road 73, which is to the west from SR 410 about 6 miles south of the town of Greenwater. The Suntop turn-off is well-marked to the left and this gravel road takes you around and about through the forest to a pass at an altitude of 4750 feet. Here there are four choices. You can continue on this road, which turns to the left and goes down slope through the forest to a creek. You can park and take a trail to the left (south), identified by a small signpost next to the road a little before you reach the top of the road. This trail leads to Fawn Ridge (Hike 119). You can take the road that branches off to the right and leads up to the Suntop Lookout; however, this road is usually closed. Or you can do as we recommend:

take the trail that leaves the road to the right a little below the pass. It climbs to the lookout at the top of Suntop along a gentle and scenic route.

The trail begins in open, sub-alpine woods, among trees ranging in size from knee-high juveniles to taller trees approaching middle age. It crosses the road in a few hundred yards but stays clear of the road for the rest of its length, which is a little under a mile. Soon the trail breaks out in the open. Mt. Rainier graces the southern horizon and, in season, the tall stocks of beargrass grace the foreground.

Above the trail isolated trees share the steep hillside with beargrass and blue lupine.

The final stretch of trail slants up onto the road near its large graveled parking area. From here one can mount the path to the well-preserved lookout cabin or one can wander along the summit ridge past picnic tables amid flowery meadows. A sign on the lookout cabin gives its altitude: 5280 feet, almost exactly the same as the altitude of Paradise Valley.

A short path south from the lookout leads to a scenic point, a perfect spot for lunch with a view of the valleys below and the sparkling white north face of Mt. Rainier. On a good day the view in the opposite direction, to the north, reveals dozens of the Cascades, from Mt. Stuart in the east to the Snoqualmie peaks in the west.

The Fawn Ridge Trail exits from the Sun Top Road just before the pass (see Hike 118 for instructions on how to get this far). There is a sign labeling it (Forest Service Trail 1183) and giving mileages, including the distance to the airstrip, which is at the opposite trailhead, 8 miles away. This trail is also called the Suntop Trail on some maps and signs.

From the trailhead the trail enters some nice second growth forest, gradually ascending along the side of the ridge. There are occasional openings in the woods, where huckleberry bushes and wildflowers can be found. The trail stays high over most of its length, reaching its highest point next to a bare knoll called Peak 5592 (because that is its elevation in feet). This point is about 2 miles from Sun Top Road. The top, reached by a short spur trail, provides a super view of Mt. Rainier.

The trail follows close to the ridge top, staying above 5000 feet for the next mile or so. Views are good, especially to the east. There are not too many users of this trail, except for mountain  bikers. It's a popular loop trip. Bikers typically take the riverside trail along the White and then ascend the Fawn Ridge Trail at one end and descend at the other. On a recent trip we first encountered a group of American bikers going clockwise, then a lone German biker going counterclockwise, and finally a brown bear who didn't tell us which way he was going.

At about 4 miles from the Sun Top Road the trail crosses the upper part of Buck Creek. This stream flows north from here, reaching the White River at a campfire amphitheater and a footbridge that leads to the Buck Creek Trail and thus to Camp Sheppard. At this crossing the trail is right at the boundary between the National Forest and National Park. It turns back to the north without entering the Park, following the contours of the Buck Creek valley. It descends slowly along Fawn Ridge, soon coming to a series of clearcuts.

Views out to the northeast open up towards the Palisades and Little Ranger Peak.

About a mile from the end, the trail crosses a logging road, which may require a bit of hunting on the other side to find the continuation of the trail. It skirts logged-off sections of forest as it continues to descend through fairly open woods.

At 3000 feet altitude it crosses mossy Doe Creek, draining from the south. The trail then enters a lowland forest with Western Hemlocks and Douglas Firs dominating the depths of a dense woodland. When the trail levels out at the bottom it encounters a maze of off-road vehicle tracks and in summer on weekends a brazen chorus of buzzing and roaring. A dash to the east through this mess brings the trail user to the south trailhead, which is at the airfield road, about one mile from the Buck Creek Road (FS 7160) and the bridge across to Highway 410.

As their name implies, the Cascades are mountains with no shortage of waterfalls. There are so many that most have no official names and many are not even marked on maps. Almost all are well worth a visit if you can find them. One exceptional falls is on Fawn Ridge, just off the Fawn Ridge-Suntop Trail. It's not exceptional because of being unusually large or spectacular, but rather because it's singled out, with an official trail to it (FS Trail 1174). It's a narrow falls on a small creek, difficult to see through the trees and almost impossible to photograph. In early summer it has a nice flow with a precipitous drop, but in late summer it comes close to disappearing, as this picture shows.

Fawn Ridge is bordered on the west by Buck Creek and on the east by Doe Creek, all having been named by someone who apparently liked deer. The Doe Falls Trail leaves the Fawn Ridge-Suntop Trail 2.2 miles above the south trailhead. The trail traverses along the ridge through second growth forest, with occasional views out to the east.

In only ½ mile the trail comes to a very steep, small valley, where the trail seems perilously perched on an unstable slope. Here is where one has the only view of Doe Falls, which is across the valley and through a partial screen of trees. Another hundred feet or so brings the hiker to a nice camp spot above the falls, near the murmuring waters of Doe Creek.

Hike 121 – Crystal Mountain Area Hikes

There are several hiking trails in the hills and valleys adjacent to the Crystal Mountain Ski Resort, which is just northeast of Mt. Rainier National Park. The resort is reached from Highway 410 on a paved road that turns left just before the highway crosses the National Park boundary. Most of the trails can be reached in summer from the resort, though there are also trailheads for some on a Forest Service road that leaves the Crystal Mountain Road to the left about 5 miles from Highway 410. The road is narrow but usually in reasonably good condition.

The first trailhead encountered from this road is the Norse Peak Trail, which is found about a quarter mile beyond the start of the gravel road. There is really no place to park near the trailhead, so it is best to park at the start of the road, where it leaves the Crystal Mountain Road, and walk to the trailhead. This trail ascends the mountain side to the left of the road, reaching Norse Peak and several other trails in a steep 5 miles.

A little over three miles from the start the road comes to a sharp switchback and its condition worsens. Here are the trailheads for Bullion Basin (2 miles) and Silver Creek (1.5 miles). It is also possible from here to reach the Pacific Crest Trail in 2.5 miles.

The trails begin rather inauspiciously as rough bulldozed tracks, but become more pleasant as they become more distant from the skiing areas.

Persons looking for a pleasant, short trail through a nice forest can try the little-known Crystal Ridge Trail, which is a ½ mile jaunt between the Crystal Mountain Road and an area of private mountain cabins hidden in the woods east of Crystal Springs. To find the lower trailhead, turn east from Highway 410 on one of the FS roads that are just downhill from the Crystal Mountain turn-off and head uphill past the cabins to the southeast corner of the cabin area. The trailhead is marked by a small sign.

The upper trailhead is found at a wide curve in the Crystal Mountain Road about 1¾ miles from its intersection with Highway 410.

Two and a half miles south of the Dalles Campground, Highway 410 encounters a paved road to the left signed "Camp Sheppard". Straight ahead up this road is the entrance to the Camp Sheppard Boy Scout camp. To the right off the road is the spur road to a Forest Service trailhead for the maze of trails that occupy the forest and the steep slopes above. The trailhead has lots of parking, a display board and a restroom.

Trail 1199

From the trailhead it is possible to reach a variety of destinations. Follow the nature trail past the pond to Trail 1199, the White River Trail, which is the main trail north and south. This is an excellent trail, passing through several different kinds of lowland forest. The way south goes through a soft and delicate woods, made up chiefly of Western Hemlocks and Douglas Firs with a graceful understory of salal and moss.

About a half mile from the trail junction the enchantment of the forest is enhanced by clumps of coralroot orchids.

After passing two intersections, both leading to the left upslope to Snoquera Falls (Trail 1167), Trail 1199 comes to a spur trail that heads right, reaching Highway 410 in about ¼ mile and accessing the Buck Creek Trail (Trail 1169)

The main trail continues on south and in about 1½ miles it encounters another junction, this one with Trail 1197, which leads steeply up the Ranger Creek valley, reaching the high plateau near Little Ranger Peak in 4.8 miles. Just before this junction Trail 1199 comes close to the highway, providing trail access, though parking on the highway shoulder is limited to not much more than one or two cars.

Trail 1199 comes to another trail junction in 1.4 miles. Here it encounters Deep Creek and a trail that goes steeply up to the east towards Noble Knob. The trail ends in another half mile at FS Road 7174, which climbs up to Corral Pass.

From the Camp Sheppard Trailhead north there are also several possibilities. After traversing above the Boy Scout Camp area, Trail 1199 passes through deep, open forest for about a mile, staying fairly level. The trees, mostly Douglas Fir, are large and there is little undergrowth.

About ¾ miles from the trailhead there is a junction with Trail 1167 to Snoquera Falls. Farther north, Trail 1199 ends. A spur trail goes left to the highway, where there is a small amount of parking, and Trail 1198 goes right to the Palisades.

The Palisades Trail switchbacks steeply up the slopes to the Ranger Plateau, reaching Little Ranger Peak in about 6 miles. Along the way it passes two waterfalls on Dalles Creek, both best viewed in early summer.

Trail 1167, the Snoquera Falls Loop

A particularly favorite trail in the Camp Sheppard Area is the Snoquera Falls Loop (Trail 1167). It can be reached from three different points on Trail 1199, two south of Camp Sheppard and one north. The following description begins at the southernmost access trail, where the highway intersects the Buck Creek Trail. From the highway it is about ¼ mile to Trail 1199 and near there is the intersection with the Snoquera Falls Loop.

The trail ascends gradually, passing through an attractive, dark forest. Along the way watch for the candy-like striped coralroot orchid. As the trail gets higher the view to the west opens up. Most conspicuous there is Suntop Mountain (Hike 119). The road to the summit is a conspicuous scar near the top.

A mile from the start of the trail at Trail 1199, the high point is reached. If you choose (wisely) to make this trip in the spring, the view at the top will be spectacular. Above you will be the vertical cliffs of the Palisades and pummeling off them will be a tower of water nearly 300 feet from top to bottom. In early spring the foliage around the trail will not yet be in leaf and a fine view can be had from the trail.

If your visit is later in the summer, the falls are still nice, but there are two difficulties: the young trees next to the trail obscure some of the view upward to the falls, and the amount of water can be small enough to look like just a thin mist (as in the adjacent picure). Adventurous hikers can consider taking an informal, steep and slippery trail to the right, just past the creek crossing, to get a better view of the falls.

314

Continuing on the Falls Loop, the trail descends along the bottom of the great cliff and then switchbacks down among some impressive Douglas Firs. The going is a little rough as the trail crosses steep talus slopes in its rapid descent. In less than a mile of this it comes to the White River Trail (number 1199) again. Turn left and follow it through the woods, past the Camp, back to the start of the loop. Watch for more orchids, especially the spotted coralroot.

Trail 1169, the Buck Creek Trail

A short trail with a surprise at the end, Trail 1169 can be reached from the White River Trail about a mile south of the Camp Sheppard Trailhead. In a quarter mile it crosses Highway 410 and plunges into the forest west of the highway (watch for the resumption of trail about a hundred yards south of the crossing, where a post is visible; it once had a trail sign mounted on it). The forest is marked by some large Douglas Firs and an occasional sunny glen. After about a half mile, the trail takes a sudden turn downwards towards the river, which it reaches in a couple of switchbacks.

The highlight of this very short trail, though, is the elegant footbridge that takes the trail across the river to the west side, where it joins the Skookum Flats Trail (number 1194).

The trails along the lower White River make excellent autumn or spring hikes, before the high country opens up. The longest is called the Skookum Flats Trail, FS Trail 1194. It extends for more than 8 miles along the west banks of the river, often rising 50 to 100 feet above the river through deep forest.

The northern Skookum Flats trailhead is located just across the bridge off Forest Service Road 73 about a quarter of a mile from Highway 410. The Road 73 turnoff is a little less that 4 miles south of Greenwater. It's usually a busy, dusty road in logging season.

The trail passes through virgin forest basically all of the way. Huge Douglas Firs and Western Red Cedars populate the deep forest. Often there are openings in the trees that reveal the meandering river below.

A highlight of the trail comes a little over two miles from the trailhead. Skookum Falls is a complex of waterfalls of Skookum Creek. Upper Skookum Falls is a spectacular waterfall, nearly 600 feet high, where the creek drops nearly vertically down the steep walls of the valley. The Upper Falls is visible from Highway 410, where there is a parking turn-out and sign. From the trail the Upper Falls are hidden by the trees, but the creek provides a nice Lower Falls as compensation. Just to the right of the trail is this pleasant cascade.

The Skookum Flats are the flat areas around the river, smoothed out by the water's action. "Skookum" is the Chinook word for "fast' or "strong".

The next point of special interest is another 2 miles south along the trail. Here there is a campfire area with an amphitheater, where campfire meetings take place, mostly by the Boy Scouts camped at Camp Sheppard. Here is also a junction with Trail 1169, the Buck Creek Trail (File 136), which crosses the river on a suspension bridge.

Another mile south on the Skookum Flats Trail brings one to Forest Service Road 7160 (the "Buck Creek Road") and another trailhead with easy access to the highway. The trail dips under the bridge and continues on farther south before finally fading out when it encounters the National Park boundary.

Other riverfront trails include shorter segments on the east side of the highway. Forest Service Trail 1204a is a pleasant 0.8 mile jaunt from the Dalles Campground north to the Huckleberry Creek bridge. Trail 1204 is a loop trip nature trail from the campground south to the river. And there are trails along the river north from the Buck Creek Road, mostly used by horse riders from the dude ranch at Buck Creek. All of these riverside trails enjoy the beauties of deep lowland forest.

Federation Forest State Park is a marvelous island of virgin forest in a sea of tree farms. It is a long narrow park, extending east-west and saddling Highway 410 and bordering on the White River. The park was established through the efforts of the Washington Federation of Women's Clubs and was dedicated in 1949. In addition to several miles of hiking trails, there are several picnic sites, an interpretive center, rest rooms and an amphitheater. In all there are 600 acres of deep virgin forest and 3½ miles of river frontage.

The park is usually reached from the northwest on Highway 410. It is 18 miles from Enumclaw. A large log sign marks the State Park boundary. There are several pullouts from the highway that serve various trailheads. The first to be encountered is just a few

hundred yards beyond the entrance log. Across the highway from Forest Service Road 7120 is a section of the historic Nachez Trail, the first route established for crossing this part of the Cascades and best preserved only in this Park. Wagon trains full of goods and settlers struggled over the mountains on this crude trail from the East.

Another trailhead is reached 0.2 miles from the log entrance. This is in two parts. The pull-out is on the right, where the trail that becomes the park's South Trail can be taken. Across the highway is another trailhead, this one for the more remote North Trail, which also traverses the park lengthwise, but is in an even more magnificent section of virgin forest.

The west nature trail is reached from a larger pull-out about 1.4 miles from the log sign. There are restrooms and a display board with park information and maps.

At the time of these photographs (June, 2003) this nature trail had not been maintained, so that there were no signs or interpretive folders (budget cut-backs had badly hurt the state parks at that time). But the trail is still very much worth following. It passes through an especially lush section of forest and goes by, for instance, an excellent example of a "nurse log", a fallen log whose decaying mass forms a nursery for many young seedlings.

The nature trail forms a loop trip about 0.5 miles long. At the far point it reaches the banks of the White River.

A very different view of the river is had from a trail that goes south from the small but excellent Interpretive Center, reached from a turn-off 2 miles from the entrance log. Several trails leave from the large parking area to the south and they reach a highly "civilized" picnic grounds, with barbeques, picnic tables, a rain shelter, restrooms and a broad lawn that stretches to the water's edge.

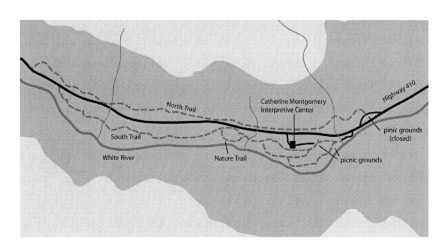

Map 16 Federation Forest

There are many trails radiating out from the visitor center, including more sections of the old Nachez Trail.

An especially nice trip is a loop trip, starting, for example, at the riverside picnic area, going east on the access road, crossing the highway near the eastern boundary of the park, where the North Trail can be found (in a now-closed small picnic grounds a few hundred yards farther east). One then can head west on the entire North Trail to the west boundary, again crossing the highway and following the South Trail back to the starting point. The entire length of the trip is about 5 miles.

Chapter 13 – The Wonderland Trail

Hike 125 – The Wonderland Trail

Every face of Mt. Rainier is different. The only way to appreciate this is to go around the mountain, looking up at it from every angle. An around-the-mountain trail, first envisioned in 1915, became a reality in the years following and by 1923 this trail had acquired its name, the Wonderland Trail. The name is fitting in the opinions of everyone who travels it (in good weather). It is now a famous trail and a popular one. It's so popular that travelers are required to have reservations to undertake it and camping along the way is restricted to backpacker "camps", of which there are 22 scattered around the mountain.

The total length of the Wonderland Trail is approximately 100 miles. The exact length depends on a couple of choices as to route on the north side of the mountain, as described below. A comfortable trip on the trail can be made in 10 days, but longer times can be taken if either a day or two of layovers is desired or if hikers are less experienced. Extra vigorous and impatient hikers do the trail in as few as 8 days.

Mt. Rainier's glacial history makes its flanks a series of high ridges bordered by deep valleys. This means that the Wonderland Trail is not a nice level 100 miles, but a series of ups and downs. Nine or ten miles of these climbs and descents are usually enough each day if carrying a heavy pack.

What follows is a day by day description of a 10-day circumnavigation on the Wonderland Trail. The coverage is brief for two reasons. First, much of the trail is already described in many of the previous chapters, as many sections of the trail make nice day hikes. Second, there exists a marvelous and very complete guide to the trail. No-one should venture to hike the Wonderland without the excellent book totally devoted to every aspect of the trail: "Discovering the Wonders of the Wonderland Trail" by Bette Filley (Dunamis House, 1992).

The description below proceeds clockwise, starting from Longmire. Of course, one can go in the other direction and can start at other access roads, as desired. The photographs here were taken in mid-August. If traveling much earlier, hikers will encounter snow on the higher stretches of trail. August usually has the most reliable weather, though September is a good choice, too, though sudden snow storms can be a surprise in the autumn.

Day One: Longmire to Devils Dream (5.9 miles)

The Wonderland Trail section from Longmire to Indian Henry's Hunting Ground via Devils Dream backpacker's camp is described in Hike 7. Devil's Dream Camp is in a pleasant woodsy area near timberline at 5000 feet elevation. There are 7 individual campsites and one group site. This is a short segment of trail, not a bad idea when you're getting used to your heavy pack and boots. It is not level, but there are stretches of easy hiking.

Day Two: Devils Dream to Klapatche Park (10.2 miles)

While the previous day was a little short of big views, this one has them in abundance. The morning enjoys the spectacular flower fields and mountain views of Indian Henry's Hunting Grounds. By mid-morning the hiker has lost altitude, steeply descending down into the valley of Tahoma Creek to encounter a highlight of the trail (for some, - a source of terror for a few). The suspension bridge crossing above the wild waters of Tahoma Creek is about `100 feet high and 250 feet long and it sways back and forth as you walk on it.

From the bridge the trail heads up again, its destination the marvelous viewpoint of Emerald Ridge (Hike 115). The mountain looms above and the Tahoma Glacier is spread out below the trail. Across the way to the north are the green meadows of the afternoon's destination, St. Andrews Park.

Then it's down again, this time to cross the South Puyallup River on a log bridge just past the trail junction with the South Puyallup Trail, which leads in 1.6 miles to Round Pass.

The South Puyallup Camp is 0.1 miles down this trail. Up again through forest the Wonderland Trail heads for the high meadows of St. Andrew's Park (Hike 117). The high point in this park is St. Andrews Lake.

A scenic mile and a half later brings the hiker to Klapatche Park (Hike 116), one of the mountain's most beautiful alpine parks, where Klapatche Camp is located. This camp is unusual for its being in an alpine parkland, whereas most camps are located lower, in forest areas so as to preserve the more delicate meadow environment. Users should be extremely careful to stay on established paths.

Day Three: Klapatche Park to Golden Lakes (7.8 miles)

The day starts with a downward trek, losing 2100 feet to reach the North Puyallup River. The trail encounters the closed West Side Highway about 2 ½ miles from Klapatche. This is the real end of the road, beyond which road construction was planned long ago but never done.

After crossing the river on a wooden bridge, the trail starts up again, first passing tiny North Puyallup Camp (three sites). About three miles from the bridge the trail enters an old burn, where dead silvery trees still stand. Topping a ridge, the trail travels through Sunset Park, reaching Golden Lakes in another two miles. There is a patrol cabin here, as well as Golden Lakes Camp, which has five nice campsites.

Day Four: Golden Lakes to Mowich Lake (10.3 miles).

The trail passes a couple of the Golden Lakes, but misses many. There are more than 30 large and small lakes in Sunset Park, all golden in the late afternoon sun. From the camp the trail travels through forest, moving nearly level along the top of a ridge. Occasional openings provide views of the valley below. At about 2 miles from the camp the trail begins to head down precipitously. Many switchbacks eventually bring it to the South Mowich River, which originates in the South Mowich and the Edmunds Glaciers.

Following a sometimes tricky crossing of this river, the trail passes the South Mowich Camp and shelter (eight campsites). A few hundred yards farther is another river to cross, the North Mowich River, which drains the glacier of the same name. Beyond this crossing the trail passes another shelter and then starts to climb towards Mowich Lake. It ascends the south slope of Paul Peak, soon coming to a trail junction with the Paul Peak Trail, which goes to the left (Hike 100). The Wonderland heads up the valley of Crater Creek and in 3.5 miles from the South Mowich River bridge it encounters another junction. To the right is the Spray Park Trail (Hike 106), which is one of two alternate

routes to the Carbon River Valley. Persons traveling this route might want to plan to go the extra mile to the Eagle Roost Camp, rather than continuing on to the rather unappealing campground at Mowich Lake.

Though its campground is not, Mowich Lake itself is quite beautiful. The largest lake in the park, it is reached by car on a gravel road from near the Carbon River Entrance.

Day Five: Mowich Lake to Carbon River Camp (8 miles)

The traditional Wonderland Trail route from Mowich Lake goes north to Ipsut Pass and then down directly to the Carbon River, reaching the river near the Ipsut Creek Campground and the Carbon River Road. An alternate, longer way (but much more scenic) is to take the trail east to glorious Spray Park (Hike 106) and then to continue up and over a high pass to Seattle Park (Hike 99) and thus down to the river close to its origin at the snout of the Carbon Glacier. This description follows the first, but a description of the Spray Park route can be found by combining Hikes 99 and 106.

From Mowich Lake the Wonderland Trail proceeds along the west bank of the lake on a wide, level trail. A mile and a half from the campground it comes to a junction with the Eunice Lake/Tolmie Peak Trail (Hikes 103 and 104). Shortly thereafter hikers arrive at

Ipsut Pass, which provides a sweeping view down into the Carbon River Valley and to the mountains to the north.From the Pass the trail simply descends, steeply at first and then more gradually as it follows Ipsut Creek. Near the valley bottom it comes to a trail junction, five miles from Mowich Lake Campground. The trail to the left goes to the Carbon River Road and the Ipsut Creek Campground. The trail to the right is the Wonderland Trail.

The Wonderland Trail along the Carbon River provides occasional views of the river and scattered views of Mt. Rainier. It is a fairly new trail, having been relocated in the 1990s, following many years of river damage to the original, which was located close (too close) to this wild and unpredictable stream. Three miles from Ipsut Creek is the Carbon River Camp, just a short distance before the Wonderland intersects the alternate trail coming down from Spray and Seattle Parks. Carbon River Camp has four sites located above the trail among the giant logs of a blowdown.

Day 6: Carbon River Camp to Mystic Lake (5 miles)

It's a short but scenic trip to Mystic Lake from Carbon River Camp. The first challenge comes only a fraction of a mile past the camp. The river crossing is another suspension bridge. It's not as high as the Tahoma Creek Bridge, but it swings in the same way, especially if more than one person is crossing at a time. The span is 205 feet.

Beyond the bridge the trail turns to the right and begins a climb along the Carbon River's east bank. The rugged Northern Crags are above the trail to the left and the grey-black snout of the Carbon Glacier looms ahead.

The Carbon Glacier is remarkable in at least two ways. Its black color is unusual and results from the fact that it cuts through a vein of coal. The debris that covers its lower slopes is rich in that black organic material. Nearby towns, such as Carbonado and Black Diamond, farther north, are named for the area's once rich coal deposits that determined their economies.

The other remarkable feature of this glacier is the fact that it reaches to such a low altitude. Its snout is at an elevation of 3600 feet, lower than that of any other glacier in the contiguous United States.

The Wonderland Trail climbs steadily up the valley above the glacier, crossing tiny Dick Creek near the precarious-looking Dick Creek Camp, perched on the side of the steep rocky slope. Dick Creek's source is a remote, high parkland called Elysian Fields, dotted with small lakes and marshes, unreachable by trail. Named for the paradise of classical Greek mythology, the Elysian Fields were supposed to be a land of perfect happiness where heroes were sent when the gods conferred immortality upon them. Few mortals visit Rainier's remote Elysian Fields, but perfect happiness may not be what they find in fly and mosquito season.

Happiness is attained, however, after trudging up the trail a couple of more miles, when the view to the south opens up and the mountain comes into view. Willis Wall, a sheer nearly vertical cliff, dominates this side of Rainier, making it one of the most spectacular faces of the mountain.

The trail passes through the lower parts of Moraine Park, which extends up and to the left onto the shoulder of a mountain appropriated named Old Desolate. It then climbs up over a pass that provides views back down the Carbon River Valley towards steep-sided Mother Mountain. A taste of what's to come is the view east from the pass, which includes the Winthrop Glacier and Burroughs Mountain looming behind it.

The trail gently drops a few hundred feet to an area of trees and meadows and soon Mystic Lake is reached (Hike 84). Mystic Lake Camp is near the far end of the lake, a few hundred yards to the right of the trail.

Day 7: Mystic Lake to Sunrise Camp (8.4 miles)

The first part of this day is dominated by the mammoth Winthrop Glacier, second largest on Rainier. After leaving Mystic Lake, the trail goes up a small rise and then steeply descends into the small valley of the West Fork of the White River, which originates above from one tongue of the Winthrop Glacier. This may be a tricky crossing, as the stream changes course at will and it's hard to keep bridges in place. Watch for cairns in the wide stream bed.

Following the east side of the West Fork, the trail loses altitude in order to pass beneath the glacier. Cliffs of debris-covered ice are on the right.

The trail swings around the bottom of the glacier, coming to a bridge over milky-white Winthrop Creek, the glacier's main outlet. This creek joins the West Fork White River, which joins the main fork of the White River north of the Park boundary. At that point the murky White River becomes the outflow of the mountain's two largest glaciers, the Winthrop and the Emmons.

The trail enters woods and switchbacks up the valley of Granite Creek, soon reaching tiny Granite Creek Camp. Above the camp there is a steep stretch and then a traverse of an open slope with glorious views of Rainier and the upper part of Burroughs Mountain.

The top of the ridge is Skyscraper Pass. Directly north is 7079 foot high Skyscraper Mountain, an easy scramble (Hike 83). Below to the east is Berkeley Park (Hike 79) and to the south is rambling Burroughs Mountain (Hike 77).

The trail now enters the Sunrise area. It swings around the upper reaches of Berkeley Park, passing through tundra-like country, where the combination of late snow melt and rocky volcanic soil makes it difficult for much more than grasses and a few hardy ground-hugging flowers to grow.

A trail junction comes next. To the left is the route to many wonders: Berkeley Park (Hike 79), Grand Park (Hike 80), Lake Eleanor (Hike 85) and the Northern Loop (Hike 78).

The trail rises gently to another trail junction. To the left is the Mt. Fremont Lookout Trail (Hike 76) and to the right is the western trail to Burroughs Mountain (Hike 77). Shortly afterward the Wonderland Trail comes to one more junction. To the right is the way down to Sunrise Camp, about a mile away. To the left is the higher trail that leads to the main settlement at Sunrise, about 2 miles away. This route has the better views.

Day 8: Sunrise Camp to Summerland (9.8 miles)

Sunrise Camp is located at the western end of the Sunrise complex, at what was formerly the lower campground of Sunrise, when it had two car campgrounds. It now has none. The upper campground is now a picnic area. The lower campground was decommissioned over 50 years ago and the areas around it are very slowly returning to a natural state.

About a mile from the Camp on the obvious main east-west trail there is a trail junction, with the continuation of the Wonderland Trail clearly indicated. The trail descends steeply on a broad, comfortable path to the White River Campground, which still exists.

Until 2001 the Wonderland Trail remained unfinished between the White River Campground and the trail up to Summerland. Hikers had to walk the campground road for a little over a mile to the Sunrise Road, turn right, cross the river on the highway bridge and then take a short section of the Wonderland Trail that paralleled the road until it came to the Summerland trail. Thanks largely to a group of volunteers and dedicated Park Service trail builders, a new section of the trail was built and now hikers stay off the road for the entire Wonderland trip.

The trail from the campground is signed next to the banks of the White River. It descends nearly to river level and then crosses on a log bridge.

The route then takes hikers into a dark forest on the north slope of Goat Island Mountain. About 1.7 miles from the river the new trail section intersects the Summerland Trail, which comes up from the left. The Wonderland Trail continues up to the right to Summerland (Hike 59). The way up to the high country is mostly in forest at first, with occasional open meadows.

The ascent is not steep but is steady, with a total elevation gain of 1900 feet from the road to the alpine country at Summerland. The route follows the valley of Fryingpan Creek most of the way, crossing several lesser streams on small bridges. There are places along the upper trail where avalanches have devastated parts of the forest. About 3 miles from the trail junction the trail crosses over Fryingpan Creek on a substantial bridge.

The last mile is steep with switchbacks. Glimpses of high meadows promise glories ahead. To the left are Summerland Camp and a stone shelter. Towering over the rolling meadows is Mt. Rainier, seen here at sunrise.

Day 9: Summerland to Nickel Creek Camp (11.3 miles)

The next to the last day of this itinerary has several highlights, including spectacular views from the trip's high point at Panhandle Gap (6750 feet in elevation). The waterfalls above Indian Bar and the unique Rainier views from Cowlitz Divide help to make this a rewarding, though long day.

The trail above Summerland quickly goes from alpine parkland to arctic tundra. The 1½ miles to the gap climb up into a snowy basin, which holds a lake that is often still frozen even in August. The trail can be snow-covered, but it is usually easy to follow either previous hikers' tracks or the frequent cairns.

At the Gap on a clear day it is possible to see almost the entire length of the state, from Mt. Baker, near the Canadian border, to Mt. Hood in Oregon. From this high point, the trail descends to the south along the side of Little Tahoma's eastern flanks, passing along a rocky shelf and over some small snow fields. A few ups and downs occur before the trail drops fairly directly to the beautiful valley at Indian Bar, 4½ miles from Summerland. There is a stone shelter and camp.

From Indian Bar the Wonderland Trail goes up a bit to reach the crest of a ridge called Cowlitz Divide, which extends from remote Cowlitz Park south for 3 scenic miles. The ridge is flower-covered in summer with vistas interrupted only by occasional clumps of alpine trees.

Leaving the ridge, the way enters forest, where it stays for the last 2½ miles to Nickel Creek Camp. Just before this descent there is a junction with the Cowlitz Divide Trail, which descends to Ollalie Camp and Ohanapecosh.

The camp at Nickel Creek is a pleasant one, set alongside the creek, which is crossed on a log bridge.

Day 10: Nickel Creek to Longmire (13.5 miles)

The last day of this Wonderland itinerary is a long one, but not especially challenging. A little less than a mile from the camp is the Box Canyon area, where the Stevens Canyon Road crosses a remarkably deep and narrow canyon on a tourist-rich bridge. The WT avoids the crowds by staying just north of the highway.

It crosses the canyon on a handsome foot bridge.

The trail completely avoids the road by going up and over the road's tunnel, providing a unique view from the trail straight down onto the highway. It then proceeds down through the forest to the bottom of Stevens Canyon, where it turns right and crosses Stevens Creek on a bridge that spans a low waterfall.

Speaking of waterfalls, two excellent examples provide special treats to ease the otherwise fairly boring trip up the valley. Both are reached after the turn-off to Maple Creek Camp, which is 3 miles from Nickel Creek Camp. The first, Sylvia Falls, is viewed from a spur trail to the right at 4.3 miles from the day's start. The second, Martha Falls, is ½ mile farther, right adjacent to the trail (Hike 33).

The Stevens Canyon Road, which has been glimpsed occasionally from below, is crossed at 6 miles from Nickel Creek. The trail nears the highway again at the top of the next slope, as both skirt around the east side of Louise Lake. They join more intimately in about a mile, when the trail reaches the Reflection Lakes and proceeds along the side of the road for a few hundred yards.

Soon the route drops down to a trail at the lake level. This is the combination of the Wonderland Trail and the Lakes Trail (Hike 26), but the latter separates off to the right at the end of the lakes. Shortly the Wonderland Trail crosses the highway and begins its descent down towards the valley of the Paradise River. The forest near the lakes is particularly attractive, fairly open and spotted with sunshine.

A junction with the Narada Falls spur trail (Hike 29) is encountered in 1.2 miles and the Paradise River Camp is passed after another 0.7 miles. Two spectacular waterfalls are passed close to the trail, Madcap Falls and Carter Falls (Hike 10), about 2.7 miles beyond Reflection Lakes.

In another mile the Nisqually River is reached and crossed on log bridges. This crossing is next to the Paradise Road and is usually busy with tourist traffic.

The Wonderland turns left abruptly to descend the final 1.6 miles to Longmire, mainly along the Nisqually River. The trail is wide and gentle and the forest is enhanced by sunny glades and glimpses of the river below to the left. The Wonderland Trail ends by emerging from the woods next to the Longmire Ranger Station.

Finally, after 10 days and 90 miles, the loop has been closed, a magnificent mountain has been circled and a famous and historic trail has been enjoyed in its entirety.

Other books in this series:

This book is also available in an expanded, full-color edition, published as a MS Word document on a CD, entitled "Mt. Rainier Hiking Trips". There are over 1000 color photographs.

Available at $14.95 from your bookstore, from Amazon.com or from the publisher.

The Mt. Baker Book

A full color digital guide to the Mt. Baker area of the North Cascades, including the setting, the landscape and a step-by-step guide to 60 hiking trails.

670 color photographs, 460 digital pages.

Published as a MS WORD document on a CD.

Available at $14.95 from your bookstore, from Amazon.com or from the publisher.